DALS
4.55

Victorian England

CONFERENCE ON BRITISH STUDIES
BIBLIOGRAPHICAL HANDBOOKS

Editor: J. JEAN HECHT

Consultant Editor: G. R. ELTON

Victorian England
1837-1901

JOSEF L. ALTHOLZ

UNIVERSITY OF MINNESOTA

CAMBRIDGE

for the Conference on British Studies

AT THE UNIVERSITY PRESS

1970

Published by the Syndics of the Cambridge University Press
Bentley House, 200 Euston Road, London N.W.1
American Branch: 32 East 57th Street, New York, N.Y.10022

Library of Congress Catalogue Card Number: 71–108097

Standard Book Number: 521 07880 6

Printed in Great Britain
at the University Printing House, Cambridge
(Brooke Crutchley, University Printer)

CONTENTS

PREFACE

This handbook is designed to serve as a basic, convenient reference guide for advanced students and professional scholars. It is a handbook in the literal sense, intended to be used as a working tool, not to be stored away on library shelves. An arbitrary editorial limit has been placed on the number of entries in order to confine the book to a size which will invite frequent use. Hence this handbook does not pretend to be a complete bibliography, although it is reasonably extensive and broadly representative of the various aspects of the history of Victorian England.

The principle of selectivity has necessarily been adopted, the chief criterion being that of potential scholarly utility. There has been some bias in favour of more recent publications. As a rule, school textbooks and merely popular works are omitted; but the line between popular and semi-scholarly writing cannot always be drawn with precision, and in many cases a popular work is the only one on a subject. Only one edition, the best or the most accessible, is cited; foreign-language works are cited in translation when a satisfactory edition in English is available. This handbook represents a fairly complete search of the literature published before 1 January 1968, with only a few entries of more recent date.

Certain areas have been excluded from the coverage of this handbook by the general editorial policy of the Bibliographical Handbooks series. Literature *per se* is not included within the scope of the series. The history of the British Empire is not covered in this volume, because the subject requires a handbook to itself. On the other hand, Irish history, which also deserves its own volume, is included here: in the century of the Union, Irish history is an integral part of the history of England. A reasonable number of entries have been devoted to Scottish history for this period, although the coverage of Scottish subjects will not be as complete as in a specialist work.

The categories employed for classifying entries are those used throughout the Bibliographical Handbooks series. All classification is arbitrary, and bibliographical classification is more arbitrary than any other; but one must employ some system. The once-seamless web of history is now divided into areas whose boundaries are constantly shifting; categories important for one period are less relevant to another; and new categories are being developed which must ultimately receive recognition. This is especially true with regard to the socio-economic aspects of modern history. Here one new field, labour history, has developed an identity and a substantial literature. Within a generation it will become customary to assign a separate category to labour history; for the present, it has been divided appropriately among existing categories, the history of trade unions being placed under Economic History. A field of urban history is recognized by many scholars; in general, works in this field have been included in Social History, but the history of local government has been placed under Constitutional and Administrative History. The history of education, a well-developed field, has been divided between Social History (for elementary, secondary and vocational education) and Intellectual History (for higher education and educational theory). More conventionally, legal history is assigned to Constitutional and Administrative History, and Intellectual History includes political and economic thought and the history of journalism. Precision in these matters is not always attainable. Works which are common to two or more categories have been placed in that to which they seem most relevant; where this is not clear, they have generally been placed in the first appropriate category, with a suitable annotation. Some cross-references have been provided in cases where a substantial number of entries relevant to one category may be found under other headings.

My conception of the role of a bibliographer is a modest one, and I do not wish to burden the reader with opinionative evaluations. The entries will therefore not be annotated, unless one of the following conditions obtains: the work is especially significant, the title does not adequately explain the contents, additional information should be supplied to the reader, or (in a few cases) I happen to have a strong opinion on the subject.

The model for my work is the first volume published in this series, Mortimer Levine's *Tudor England*. A comparison with that work may indicate some significant trends in the historiography of Victorian England. Most notable is the burgeoning and professional development of social and economic history, appropriate to the industrial society of the period, but also in part explained by the abundance of sources and statistics. By contrast, constitutional history is much less emphasized, although there is a revival of specialized studies in administrative history. The fact that the Reformation took place in the sixteenth, not the nineteenth, century explains the smaller number of entries in religious history, a field which in reality receives ample attention despite its less central role. The extension of literacy and the growth of the press may account for the proliferation of intellectual history, and there is no need to search for the reason for the development of the history of science, which is in fact becoming a distinct discipline. Finally, it is evident that, notwithstanding these trends, political history retains its pre-eminence for the largest number of historians.

Editions of printed sources are of rather less importance for the more recent periods of history. For Victorian history, the most important printed sources—Parliamentary Papers and the periodical press—are too numerous to be cited individually, although reference is made to various guides for their use. One other sort of printed source must be treated with restraint: the autobiography, of which Victorians were inordinately fond, but of which only the most important examples can be cited. Indeed the biographical mode of expression is unusually prominent in Victorian historiography. Perhaps the highest form of literature known to the Victorians was the two-volume 'Life and Letters'. Many of these are works of memorial sentiment rather than of history, yet they may be important because of documentary or anecdotal material which they contain. The vogue of biography has continued into the twentieth century, and this genre may have an undue prominence in the literature. This may well be inevitable; to many people, writing about the Victorians is little more than gossiping about one's grandparents. Perhaps this, like the essay (which continues as an English, but not American, genre), is a necessary counterpoise to the mass of monographic literature produced by professional historians.

The compilation of this handbook was made possible by a short leave of absence and a research grant from the University of Minnesota. It could not have been completed without the aid of my research assistants, Helen Hebrank and Charles Panayides. Among my colleagues, I am indebted to David Kieft and (for the history of science) to Leonard Wilson. The manuscript was read and helpfully criticized by Professor J. B. Conacher of the University of Toronto, with the assistance of his colleague, Richard Helmstadter. Most important of all is my indebtedness to the General Editor, Dr J. Jean Hecht, for his encouragement, guidance and occasional correction.

JOSEF L. ALTHOLZ

Minneapolis, Minnesota
January 1969

ABBREVIATIONS

AgHR	*Agricultural History Review*
AHR	*American Historical Review*
BIHR	*Bulletin of the Institute of Historical Research*
Camb. Hist. J.	*Cambridge Historical Journal*
CHBE	*The Cambridge History of the British Empire*, ed. John H. Rose, Arthur P. Newton and Ernest A. Benians, Cambridge, 1929–59
CMH	*The Cambridge Modern History*, ed. Lord Acton *et al.*, Cambridge, 1902–26
CQR	*Church Quarterly Review*
EcHR	*Economic History Review*
EHR	*English Historical Review*
Ess. Ec. Hist.	*Essays in Economic History*, ed. Eleanore M. Carus-Wilson, 1954–62
Hist. J.	*Historical Journal*
Id. & Inst.	*Ideas and Institutions of Victorian Britain: essays in honour of George Kitson Clark*, ed. Robert Robson, 1967
IHS	*Irish Historical Studies*
IRSH	*International Review of Social History*
JBS	*Journal of British Studies*
JEH	*Journal of Ecclesiastical History*
JEcH	*Journal of Economic History*
JHI	*Journal of the History of Ideas*
JMH	*Journal of Modern History*
NCMH	*The New Cambridge Modern History*, ed. George N. Clark *et al.*, Cambridge, 1957–
PMLA	*Publications of the Modern Language Association*
PP	*Past and Present*
SHR	*Scottish Historical Review*
TRHS	*Transactions of the Royal Historical Society*
VS	*Victorian Studies*

EXPLANATORY NOTES

1. When no place of publication is given for a book, its place of publication is London. When a book appeared both in England and elsewhere, the English place of publication is normally given.

2. For printed sources where there are no authors' names to be given, editors' names precede titles of works.

I BIBLIOGRAPHIES

1 Amano, Keitaro (ed.). *Bibliography of the classical economics.* Tokyo, 1961–4, 5 vols.
2 *Annual bibliography of the history of British art.* 1936–. Begins with publications of 1934.
3 *Annual bulletin of historical literature.* 1912–. Begins with publications of 1911.
4 *A bibliography of the history of Wales.* 2nd ed., Cardiff, 1962.
5 *A bibliography of parliamentary debates of Great Britain.* 1956.
6 Brophy, Jacqueline. 'Bibliography of British labor and radical journals, 1880–1914', *Labor History*, 3 (Winter 1962), 103–26.
7 Carty, James (ed.). *Bibliography of Irish history, 1870–1911.* Dublin, 1940.
8 Chrimes, Stanley B. and Ivan A. Roots (eds.). *English constitutional history: a select bibliography* (Helps for Students of History, no. 58). 1958.
9 Clive, John. 'British history, 1870–1914, reconsidered: recent trends in the historiography of the period', in Elizabeth C. Furber (ed.). *Changing views on British history: essays on historical writing since 1939.* Cambridge, Mass., 1966, pp. 264–83. Excellent discussion of works published 1939–63. Continues (29).
10 'Critical bibliography of the history of science and its cultural influences', *Isis*, 1– (1913–). Title has varied.
11 *English local history handlist* (Historical Association, special series, S2). Rev. ed., 1952.
12 Frewer, Louis B. (ed.). *Bibliography of historical writings published in Great Britain and the Empire, 1940–1945.* Oxford, 1947.
13 Gross, Charles (ed.). *A bibliography of British municipal history.* 2nd ed., ed. Geoffrey H. Martin. Leicester, 1966.
14 Harrison, Brian. 'Drink and sobriety in England 1815–1872: a critical bibliography', *IRSH*, 12 (no. 2, 1967), 204–76.
15 Howe, George F. *et al.* (eds.). *The American Historical Association's guide to historical literature.* New York, 1961. Highly selective general bibliography, somewhat limited on Victorian England. Supersedes the earlier *Guide to historical literature* (New York, 1931).
16 *International bibliography of historical sciences.* Paris, 1930–. Begins with publications of 1926; vol. XXXII, published in 1966, covers publications of 1963.
17 Kellaway, William (ed.). *Bibliography of historical works issued in the United Kingdom, 1957–60.* 1962.
18 —— *Bibliography of historical works issued in the United Kingdom, 1961–65.* 1967.
19 Kelly, Thomas (ed.). *A select bibliography of adult education in Great Britain, including works published to the end of the year 1961.* 2nd ed., 1962. Kept up to date by annual supplements in the Sept. issues of the *Yearbook* of the National Institute of Adult Education.
20 Lancaster, Joan C. (ed.). *Bibliography of historical works issued in the United Kingdom, 1946–1956.* 1957.
21 McGregor, Oliver R. 'The social position of women in England, 1850–1914: a bibliography', *British Journal of Sociology*, 6 (Mar. 1955), 48–60.
22 Manwaring, George E. (ed.). *A bibliography of British naval history: a bibliographical and historical guide to printed and manuscript sources.* 1930. Printed sources include articles but not books.
23 Matthews, William (ed.). *British autobiographies: an annotated bibliography of British autobiographies published or written before 1851.* Berkeley, 1955.
24 —— *British diaries: an annotated bibliography of British diaries between 1442 and 1942.* Berkeley, 1950.
25 Milne, A. Taylor (ed.). *Writings on British history.* 1937–60, 8 vols. Covers books and articles published from 1934 to 1945.
26 Mulvey, Helen F. 'Modern Irish history since 1940: a bibliographical survey (1600–1922)', in Elizabeth C. Furber (ed.). *Changing views on British*

> *history: essays on historical writing since 1939.* Cambridge, Mass., 1966, pp. 345–78.

27 'Other recent publications', *AHR*, 42– (1936–). Title varies. The section on 'Great Britain, Commonwealth and Ireland' in each issue is useful although incomplete in its listing of articles.

28 Ottley, George (ed.). *A bibliography of British railway history.* 1966.

29 Prouty, Roger W. 'England and Wales, 1820–1870, in recent historiography: a selective bibliography', in Elizabeth C. Furber (ed.). *Changing views on British history: essays on historical writing since 1939.* Cambridge, Mass., 1966, pp. 234–63. Covers works published 1939–60; not always accurate. See (9).

30 Roach, John (ed.). *A bibliography of modern history.* Cambridge, 1967. Correlated with the *New Cambridge Modern History.*

31 Slack, Robert C. (ed.). *Bibliographies of studies in Victorian literature for the ten years 1955–1964.* Urbana, Ill., 1967. Reprints the annual bibliographies in *Modern Philology* (1956–7) and *VS* (1958–65). See (32).

32 'Victorian Bibliography for 1957–', *VS*, 1– (June 1958–). The most complete annual bibliography for books; useful but less complete for articles.

33 Webb, Robert K. *English history, 1815–1914* (Service Center for Teachers of History, no. 64). Washington, 1967.

II CATALOGUES, GUIDES, AND HANDBOOKS

34 Boase, Frederic (ed.). *Modern English biography: containing many thousand concise memoirs of persons who have died between the years 1851–1900, with an index of the most interesting matter.* 1965, 6 vols. Originally published Truro, 1892–1921. More but briefer entries than (79).

35 *British almanac of the Society for the Diffusion of Useful Knowledge.* 1828–1913, 87 vols. Title varies. Annual, with supplementary *Companion.*

36 British Museum. *Catalogue of printed books, supplement: newspapers published in Great Britain and Ireland, 1801–1900.* 1905.

37 —— *The catalogues of the manuscript collections.* 1962. Lists the major collections and their catalogues. The British Museum and the Public Record Office are the two largest manuscript repositories for the Victorian period.

38 —— *General catalogue of printed books.* 1959–66, 263 vols. *Additions,* 1964–. The photolithographic edition goes to 1955. A ten-year supplement, 1956–65, is in progress.

39 Buttress, Frederick A. (ed.). *Agricultural periodicals of the British Isles, 1681–1900, and their location.* Cambridge, 1950.

40 *Census reports of Great Britain, 1801–1931* (Guides to Official Sources, II). 1951.

41 Cheney, Christopher R. (ed.). *Handbook of dates for students of English history* (Royal Historical Society guides and handbooks, no. 4). 1961.

42 Clark, George S. R. Kitson and Geoffrey R. Elton (eds.). *Guide to the research facilities in history in the universities of Great Britain and Ireland.* 2nd ed., Cambridge, 1965. Indicates the research possibilities of each university.

43 Crone, John S. (ed.). *A concise dictionary of Irish biography.* Rev. ed., Dublin, 1937.

44 Cushing, Helen G. and Adah V. Morris (eds.). *Nineteenth century readers' guide to periodical literature, 1890–1899, with supplementary indexing, 1900–1922.* New York, 1944, 2 vols.

45 Eager, Alan R. *A guide to Irish bibliographical material.* 1964.

46 *The English catalogue of books,* I–VII. 1864–1906. Lists all books published from 1835.

47 Ford, Percy and Grace. *A breviate of parliamentary papers, 1900–1916.* Oxford, 1957.

48 Ford, Percy and Grace. *A guide to parliamentary papers: what they are and how to find them, how to use them.* Oxford, 1955. A useful guide.

49 —— *Select list of British parliamentary papers 1833–1899.* Oxford, 1953. Invaluable.

50 *General alphabetical index to the bills, reports, estimates, accounts and papers, 1852–1899.* 1909. Combines the decennial volumes (similarly entitled), but difficult to use because it omits the command paper numbers. The annual lists must be consulted; see (65).

51 *General index to the accounts and papers, reports of commissioners, estimates, etc., 1801–1852.* 1938.

52 Gilson, Julius P. (ed.). *A student's guide to the manuscripts of the British Museum* (Helps for Students of History, no. 31). 1920.

53 Griffith, Margaret. 'Short guide to the Public Record Office of Ireland', *Irish Historical Studies*, 8 (Mar. 1952), 45–58.

54 *Guide to the contents of the Public Record Office.* 1963, 2 vols. The starting-point for research at the Public Record Office. Replaces Montague S. Giuseppi (ed.). *A guide to the manuscripts preserved in the Public Record Office.* 1923–4. 2 vols.

55 *Guide to the historical publications of the societies of England and Wales* (*BIHR*, supplements I–XIII). 1929–46.

56 Hall, Hubert (ed.). *A repertory of British archives*, pt. I. 1920. Indicates where public records may be found.

57 *Historical abstracts 1775–1945. A quarterly of abstracts of historical articles appearing currently in periodicals the world over.* Santa Barbara, Cal., 1955–. A useful abstracting service, with a subject index.

58 Historical Manuscripts Commission. *Record repositories in Great Britain.* 1964. A very complete pamphlet.

59 Houghton, Walter E. (ed.). *The Wellesley index to Victorian periodicals 1824–1900*, I. Toronto, 1966. Other volumes to follow. A list of all articles in selected monthlies and quarterlies, with attributions of authorship; also bibliographies of authors and a list of pseudonyms. The basic tool for periodicals research.

60 Hugh, Father. *Nineteenth century pamphlets at Pusey House; an introduction for the prospective user.* 1961. Sources for the history of Anglo-Catholicism.

61 *Indexes to bills and reports, 1801–52*, I, *General index. Bills*, II, *Reports of select committees*, III, *Accounts and papers, reports of commissioners, estimates, etc.* 1853. Vol. III reprinted 1938; see (51).

62 Irwin, Raymond and Ronald Staveley (eds.). *The libraries of London.* 2nd ed., 1961. Library resources in London.

63 Jones, Hilda V. (ed.). *Catalogue of parliamentary papers, 1801–1900, with a few of earlier date.* 1904.

64 *List of cabinet papers, 1880–1914* (Public Record Office Handbooks, no. 4). 1964.

65 *List of the bills, reports, estimates and accounts and papers.* 1801–. An annual numbered list.

66 Lloyd, John E. and Robert T. Jenkins (eds.). *The dictionary of Welsh biography down to 1940.* Oxford, 1959.

67 Muddiman, Joseph G. (ed.). *Tercentenary handlist of English and Welsh newspapers, magazines and reviews, 1660–1920.* 1920. Often referred to as the *Times tercentenary handlist.*

68 Munby, Alan N. L. *Cambridge college libraries: aids for research students.* 2nd ed., Cambridge, 1962.

69 *National register of archives.* 2nd ed., 1947–. Useful for local archives.

70 *The newspaper press directory.* 1846–. Annual; often referred to as *Mitchell's directory.*

71 Palmer, Samuel (ed.). *Index to 'The Times' newspaper.* Corsham, 1868–1943. Quarterly volumes, covering 1790–1941.

72 Poole, William F. (ed.). *Poole's index to periodical literature, 1802–1906.* Boston, 1887–1906, 6 vols. A subject index only.

73 Powicke, Frederick M. and Edmund B. Fryde (eds.). *Handbook of British chronology* (Royal Historical Society guides and handbooks, no. 2). 2nd ed., 1961.

74 *The prime ministers' papers. A survey of the privately preserved papers of those statesmen who held the office of prime minister.* 1968.

75 *Public Record Office: lists and indexes.* 1892–1936, 55 vols. *Supplementary series,* 1961–. Detailed lists and indexes of source materials at the Public Record Office.

76 *Reports of the Royal Commission on Public Records.* 3 vols., in *Parliamentary papers,* 1912–13, 1914, 1919. Reports on national and local records.

77 Somerville, Robert (ed.). *Handlist of record publications* (British Record Association, pamphlet no. 3). 1951.

78 *The statesman's year book; statistical and historical annual of the states of the world.* 1864–. Extensive section on Britain.

79 Stephen, Leslie and Sidney Lee. *The dictionary of national biography, from the earliest time to 1900.* 1885–1900, 63 vols. *Supplement.* 1901, 3 vols. Both reissued 1908–9, 22 vols. *Supplement, 1901–11.* 1920. *Supplement, 1912–1921.* 1927. *Supplement, 1922–1930.* 1937. *Supplement, 1931–1940.* 1949. *Supplement, 1941–1950.* 1959. The great British biographical dictionary. A new *DNB* is projected. See also *The concise dictionary of national biography,* I: *From the beginnings to 1900.* 1953. An epitome, with corrigenda. Additional corrigenda are published in *BIHR.*

80 *The subject index to periodicals.* 1915–61. The best guide to periodicals containing articles on British history. Known since 1962 as the *British humanities index.* 1962–.

81 Temperley, Harold W. V. and Lillian M. Penson. *A century of diplomatic blue books, 1814–1914.* Cambridge, 1938. Reissued, 1966.

82 Thomson, Theodore R. (ed.). *A catalogue of British family histories.* 1935.

83 Wardle, D. B. 'Sources for the history of railways at the Public Record Office', *Journal of Transport History,* 2 (Nov. 1956), 214–34.

84 *Whitaker's almanac.* 1874–. Annual; a valuable work of general reference.

85 *Who's who: an annual biographical dictionary.* 1849–. For persons who died after 1896, entries are cumulated in *Who was who,* I, *1897–1915.* 4th ed., 1953. II, *1916–28.* 1929. III, *1929–40.* 1941. IV, *1941–50.* 1952.

86 Williams, Judith Blow. *A guide to the printed materials for English social and economic history, 1750–1850.* New York, 1926, 2 vols.

87 Winfield, Percy H. *The chief sources of English legal history.* Cambridge, Mass., 1925. The best introduction to the subject.

III GENERAL SURVEYS

88 Arnstein, Walter L. *Britain yesterday and today: 1830 to the present* (A History of England, IV). Boston, 1966.

89 Ausubel, Herman. *The late Victorians: a short history.* New York, 1955. Emphasizes the 'great depression'; with documents.

90 Briggs, Asa. *The age of improvement, 1783–1867.* 1959. A good survey by a leading scholar.

91 —— *Victorian people: some reassessments of people, institutions, ideas, and events, 1851–1867.* 1954. A collection of illuminating essays. The American edition (Chicago, 1955) contains additional elements.

92 Burn, William L. *The age of equipoise: a study of the mid-Victorian generation.* 1964. A stimulating interpretation of the period 1850–67, especially important for administrative and social history.

93 Butler, James R. M. *A history of England, 1815–1939.* 1960. An excellent brief survey; originally published 1928.

94 Clark, George S. R. Kitson. *An expanding society: Britain 1830–1900.* 1967. Interpretative lectures.

95 —— *The making of Victorian England.* 1962. The Ford Lectures for 1960 constitute the most important single work on Victorian England since Young: a manifesto of revisionism, surveying recent research and projecting directions for the future.

96 Derry, John W. *Reaction and reform: England in the early nineteenth century*, *1793–1868*. 1963.

97 Ensor, Robert C. K. *England 1870–1914* (Oxford History of England, XIV). Oxford, 1936. One of the best volumes in this series.

98 Gretton, Richard H. *A modern history of the English people, 1880–1922*. 1930, 3 vols. Vols. I–II relate to this period.

99 Halévy, Elie. *A history of the English people in the nineteenth century*, III, *The triumph of reform 1830–1841*, IV, *The age of Peel and Cobden*, V, *Imperialism and the rise of labour*, tr. Edward I. Watkin, 2nd ed., 1949–52. This six-volume series by a French scholar is a masterpiece. Although Halévy's interpretations are subject to revision, there is no work comparable in scope and distinction. Vol. IV, though incomplete, contains a useful section on religion in 1851. The period 1851–95 is not covered.

100 Jarman, Thomas L. *Democracy and world conflict, 1868–1962: a history of modern Britain*. 1963.

101 Macdonald, Donald F. *The age of transition: Britain in the nineteenth and twentieth centuries*. 1967.

102 Marriott, John A. R. *England since Waterloo*. 15th ed., 1954. See also *Modern England, 1885–1945; a history of my own times*. 4th ed., 1960.

103 Paul, Herbert. *A history of modern England*. 5 vols., 1904–6. A partisan Liberal account, much dated.

104 Pelling, Henry. *Modern Britain, 1885–1955*. Edinburgh, 1960.

105 Petrie, Charles A. *The Victorians*. 1960.

106 Smellie, Kingsley B. S. *Great Britain since 1688, a modern history*. Ann Arbor, 1962.

107 Thomson, David. *England in the nineteenth century* (Pelican History of England, VIII). Harmondsworth, 1950.

108 Trevelyan, George M. *British history in the nineteenth century and after*. 2nd ed., 1937. In the best Whig tradition.

109 Walpole, Spencer. *A history of England from the conclusion of the great war in 1815*. New ed., 1890, 6 vols. The earliest general survey.

110 —— *The history of twenty-five years*. 1904–8, 4 vols. Covers 1856–80.

111 Ward, Thomas Humphry (ed.). *The reign of Queen Victoria; a survey of fifty years of progress*. 1887, 2 vols. How the Victorians viewed their age.

112 Webb, Robert K. *Modern England; from the eighteenth century to the present*. New York, 1968. Perhaps the best survey for American use; interesting appendices.

113 Wood, Anthony. *Nineteenth century Britain, 1815–1914*. 1960. A sixth-form text-book that deserves a better audience.

114 Woodward, E. Llewellyn. *The age of reform, 1815–1870* (Oxford History of England, XIII). 2nd ed., 1962. Useful bibliography.

115 Young, George M. (ed.). *Early Victorian England*. Oxford, 1934, 2 vols. This collection of essays is a landmark in the revaluation of the Victorian era.

116 Young, George M. *Victorian England: portrait of an age*. 2nd ed., Oxford, 1953. This classic, originally published 1936, is an erudite and wise interpretation and a literary gem.

IV CONSTITUTIONAL AND ADMINISTRATIVE HISTORY

1 Printed sources

117 Bagehot, Walter. *The English constitution*. 2nd ed., 1872. A Victorian classic, still valuable as an analysis of the political system. The introduction to the 2nd ed. takes account of the effects of the 1867 reform.

118 Barker, William A. *et al.* (eds.). *A general history of England: documents*, II, *1832–1950*. 1953.

119 Benson, Arthur C. and Reginald B. Brett, 2nd Viscount Esher (eds.). *The letters of Queen Victoria, a selection from Her Majesty's correspondence between the years 1837 and 1861.* 1907, 3 vols. The first series of the Queen's letters, an indispensable source. See (121) and (122).

120 Bolitho, Hector (ed.). *Further letters of Queen Victoria, from the archives of the house of Brandenburg-Prussia,* tr. Mrs John S. (Crystal H.) Pudney and Arthur P. J. C. J. Gore, Viscount Sudley, 1938.

121 Buckle, George E. (ed.). *The letters of Queen Victoria, a selection from Her Majesty's correspondence and journal between the years 1862 and 1885.* 1926-8, 3 vols. The second series.

122 —— *The letters of Queen Victoria, a selection from Her Majesty's correspondence and journal between the years 1886 and 1901.* 1930-2, 3 vols. The third series.

123 Connell, Brian (ed.). *Regina vs. Palmerston; the correspondence between Queen Victoria and her foreign and prime minister, 1837-1865.* 1962.

124 Costin, William C. and J. Steven Watson (eds.). *The law and working of the constitution,* II, *1784-1914.* 1952. A useful collection of basic documents.

125 Edmonds, E. L. and O. P. (eds.). *I was there: the memoirs of Hugh S. Tremenheere.* Eton, 1966. Diary and letters of a pioneer inspector of mines and schools. See (301).

126 *The English reports.* Edinburgh, 1900-30, 176 vols. Law reports, 1220-1865. Replaces several earlier compilations, retaining the original paging.

127 Guedalla, Philip (ed.). *The Queen and Mr Gladstone.* 1933, 2 vols. A selection of their correspondence, with interesting commentary.

128 Hardcastle, Mary S. (ed.). *Life of John, Lord Campbell, lord high chancellor of Great Britain; consisting of a selection from his autobiography, diary and letters.* 2 vols., 1881.

129 Jagow, Curt (ed.). *Letters of the Prince Consort, 1831-1861,* tr. Edgar T. S. Dugdale. 1938.

130 *Journals of the House of Commons,* XCII-CLV. 1837-1900.

131 *Journals of the House of Lords,* LXIX-CXXXII. 1837-1900.

132 Keir, David Lindsay and Frederick Henry Lawson (eds.). *Cases in constitutional law.* 4th ed., 1954. A basic collection.

133 *The law list.* 1841-. Annual list of judges, barristers and solicitors.

134 *The law reports.* 1865-. Several series, one for each court. Continues (126).

135 London County Council. *The housing question in London. Being an account of the housing work done by the Metropolitan Board of Works and the London County Council between the years 1855 and 1900 . . .* 1900.

136 *The municipal year book and public utilities directory, 1897-.* 1897-. Annual.

137 *The public general statutes.* 1866-1925, 63 vols. Texts of public acts of each session. Continues (141).

138 *Reports of state trials.* New series, 1888-98, 8 vols.

139 Selborne, Roundell Palmer, 1st Earl of. *Memorials,* ed. Lady Sophia Palmer. 1896-8, 4 vols.

140 *The statutes, from the twentieth year of King Henry the Third to the tenth chapter of the twelfth, thirteenth, and fourteenth years of King George the Sixth, A.D. 1235-1948.* 3rd ed., 1950-.

141 *The statutes of the United Kingdom of Great Britain and Ireland.* 1807-65, 59 vols. Continues *The statutes at large.*

142 Stephenson, Carl and Frederick G. Marcham (eds.). *Sources of English constitutional history.* New York, 1937. A handy edition of basic documents.

143 Violette, Eugene M. (ed.). *English constitutional documents since 1832.* New York, 1936.

144 Young, George M. and W. D. Handcock (eds.). *English historical documents, 1833-1874* (English Historical Documents, XII, pt. 1). 1956. A substantial general collection.

2 Surveys

145 Holdsworth, William S. *A history of English law,* XIV-XVI, ed. Arthur L. Goodhart and Harold G. Hanbury. 3rd ed., 1964-6. The fullest legal history of England, a great work of reference.

146 Keir, David Lindsay. *Constitutional history of modern Britain, 1485–1951.* 8th ed., 1966. An excellent textbook.
147 Keith, A. Berriedale. *The constitutional history of England from Victoria to George VI.* 1940.
148 Marcham, Frederick G. *A constitutional history of modern England, 1485 to the present.* New York, 1960.
149 Plucknett, Theodore F. T. *A concise history of the common law.* 5th ed., 1956. The best short history.
150 Smellie, Kingsley B. *A hundred years of English government.* 2nd ed., 1951. The best general account of governmental growth since 1832.

3 Monographs
(See also sec. v, pt. 3, below.)

151 Abel-Smith, Brian and Robert Stevens. *Lawyers and the courts: a sociological study of the English legal system, 1750–1965.* 1967. Somewhat opinionated.
152 Abramovitz, Moses and Vera F. Eliasberg. *The growth of public employment in Great Britain.* Princeton, 1957.
153 Allyn, Emily. *Lords versus Commons, a century of conflict and compromise, 1830–1930.* 1931.
154 Anson, William R. *The law and custom of the constitution.* 10th ed., Oxford, 1959, 2 vols. A standard textbook, first published 1886–92.
155 Ball, Nancy. *Her Majesty's inspectorate, 1839–1849.* Edinburgh, 1963.
156 Birks, Michael. *Gentlemen of the law.* 1960. A history of the solicitors' profession.
157 Brand, Jeanne L. *Doctors and the state: the British medical profession and government action in public health, 1870–1912.* Baltimore, 1965.
158 Brockington, Colin F. *Medical officers of health, 1848–1855.* 1957.
159 Cecil, Algernon. *Queen Victoria and her prime ministers.* 1953.
160 Chubb, Basil. *The control of public expenditure; financial committees of the House of Commons.* Oxford, 1952.
161 Clarke, John J. A. *A history of local government of the United Kingdom.* 1955.
162 Clifford, Frederick. *A history of private bill legislation.* 1885–7, 2 vols.
163 Clokie, Hugh M. and Joseph W. Robinson. *Royal commissions of inquiry; the significance of investigations in British politics.* Stanford, 1937.
164 Cohen, Emmeline W. *The growth of the British civil service, 1780–1939.* 1941. The best survey of the subject.
165 Cooke, Colin A. *Corporation, trust and company: an essay in legal history.* Manchester, 1950.
166 Critchley, Thomas A. *A history of police in England and Wales, 900–1966.* 1967.
167 Dicey, Albert V. *Introduction to the study of the law of the constitution.* 10th ed., 1959. A classic.
168 —— *Lectures on the relation between law and public opinion in England during the nineteenth century.* 2nd ed., 1914. Dicey's concept of a struggle between individualism and interventionism has been important in framing the terms of historical discussion of this period.
169 Dilnot, George. *The story of Scotland Yard.* 1926.
170 Edmonds, E. L. *The school inspector.* 1962.
171 Emden, Cecil S. *The people and the constitution: being a history of the development of the people's influence in British government.* 2nd ed., Oxford, 1956.
172 Fifoot, Cecil H. S. *Judge and jurist in the reign of Victoria.* 1959. Brief lectures.
173 Finer, Herman. *English local government.* 4th ed., 1950. A standard work.
174 Formoy, Ronald R. *The historical foundations of modern company law.* 1923.
175 Frazer, William M. *A history of English public health, 1834–1939.* 1950.
176 Gibbon, I. Gwilym and Reginald W. Bell. *History of the London County Council.* 1939.
177 Graves, Robert. *They hanged my saintly Billy.* 1957. The *cause célèbre* of William Palmer, 1856.
178 Graveson, Ronald H. and Francis R. Crane (eds.). *A century of family law 1857–1957.* 1957. From a lawyer's point of view.

179 Greaves, Harold R. G. *The civil service in the changing state; a survey of civil service reform and the implications of a planned economy on public administration in England.* 1947.

180 Griffith, Llewelyn W. *The British civil service 1854–1954.* 1954. A good short study.

181 —— *A hundred years: the Board of Inland Revenue 1849–1949.* 1949.

182 Hall, Henry L. *The Colonial Office: a history.* New York, 1937. Covers 1835–85.

183 Hardie, Frank. *The political influence of Queen Victoria, 1861–1901.* 1935. An important monograph.

184 Harrison, Michael. *Painful details: twelve Victorian scandals.* 1962. Cases, 1846–96, in family law and inheritance.

185 Hedges, Robert Y. and Allan Winterbottom. *The legal history of trade unionism.* 1930.

186 Hinde, Richard S. E. *The British penal system, 1773–1950.* 1951.

187 Howard, Derek L. *The English prisons: their past and their future.* 1960.

188 Humphreys, Betty V. *Clerical unions in the civil service.* 1958.

189 Hutchins, B. Leigh and Amy Harrison [Spencer]. *A history of factory legislation.* 3rd ed., 1926.

190 Ilbert, Courtenay P. *Legislative methods and forms.* Oxford, 1901.

191 Jenks, Edward. *An outline of English local government.* 2nd ed., 1907.

192 Jennings, W. Ivor. *Cabinet government.* Cambridge, 1936. An admirable and exhaustive study.

193 Keith, Arthur Berriedale. *The British cabinet system*, ed. N. H. Gibbs. 2nd ed., 1953.

194 Keith-Lucas, Bryan. *The English local government franchise: a short history.* Oxford, 1952.

195 Kelsall, Roger K. *Higher civil servants in Britain from 1870 to the present day.* 1955.

196 Kingsley, John D. *Representative bureaucracy: an interpretation of the British civil service.* Yellow Springs, Ohio, 1944.

197 Laski, Harold J. *The British cabinet, a study of its personnel, 1801–1924* (Fabian Tract no. 223). 1928. Contains useful statistical information.

198 Laski, Harold J., W. Ivor Jennings and William A. Robson (eds.). *A century of municipal progress, 1835–1935.* 1935.

199 Lee, John M. *Social leaders and public persons: a study of county government in Cheshire since 1888.* Oxford, 1963.

200 Lewis, Richard A. *Edwin Chadwick and the public health movement, 1832–1854.* 1952.

201 Low, Sidney. *The governance of England.* 1904. An old standard work.

202 Lowell, A. Lawrence. *The government of England.* New ed., New York, 1912, 2 vols.

203 MacDonagh, Oliver. *A pattern of government growth, 1800–1860: the Passenger Acts and their enforcement.* 1961. An important study of the regulation of the emigrant passenger traffic, from which MacDonagh derives a model of legislative and administrative development.

204 McDowell, Robert B. *The Irish administration, 1801–1914* (Studies in Irish History, 2nd ser., II). 1964.

205 Mackintosh, John P. *The British Cabinet.* 1962.

206 Marriott, John A. R. *Queen Victoria and her ministers.* 1933.

207 May, Erskine. *A treatise on the law, privileges, proceedings, and usage of parliament*, ed. T. Lonsdale Webster. 12th ed., 1917. A useful manual.

208 Moses, Robert. *The civil service of Great Britain.* New York, 1914.

209 Newsholme, Arthur. *The Ministry of Health.* 1925. Deals also with its nineteenth-century predecessors.

210 Parris, Henry. *Government and the railways in nineteenth-century Britain.* 1965.

211 Petrie, Charles. *The modern British monarchy.* 1961.

212 Prouty, Roger W. *The transformation of the Board of Trade, 1830–1855.* 1957.

213 Radzinowicz, Leon. *A history of English criminal law and its administration from 1750.* 1948–57, 3 vols.

214 Radzinowicz, Leon. *Sir James Fitzjames Stephen, 1829–1894, and his contribution to the development of criminal law.* 1957.
215 Redford, Arthur, assisted by Ina S. Russell. *The history of local government in Manchester.* 1939–40, 3 vols.
216 Redlich, Josef. *Local government in England,* ed. Francis W. Hirst. 1903, 2 vols.
217 Reith, Charles. *A new study of police history.* 1956.
218 Roberts, David. *Victorian origins of the British welfare state.* New Haven, 1960. A major study of early Victorian administrative history.
219 Robinson, Howard. *The British Post Office, a history.* 1948.
220 Robson, William A. *The development of local government.* 3rd ed., 1954.
221 Rose, Gordon. *The struggle for penal reform: the Howard League and its predecessors* (The Library of Criminology, III). 1961.
222 Ruggles-Brise, Evelyn J. *The English prison system.* 1921.
223 St John-Stevas, Norman. *Obscenity and the law.* 1956. A provocative essay on the law of pornography.
224 Simon, John. *English sanitary institutions, reviewed in their course of development, and in some of their political and social relations.* 2nd ed., 1897. By a great reformer and administrator.
225 Simon, Shena D. *A century of city government: Manchester 1838–1938.* 1938.
226 Simpson, Alfred W. B. *An introduction to the history of the land law.* 1961.
227 Smellie, Kingsley B. *A history of local government.* 3rd ed., 1957. A useful summary.
228 Thomas, John A. *The House of Commons, 1832–1901: a study of its economic and functional character.* Cardiff, 1939.
229 Thomas, Maurice W. *The early factory legislation; a study in legislative and administrative evolution.* Leigh-on-Sea, 1948. Covers 1831–53.
230 Traill, Henry D. *Central government,* ed. Henry Craik. Rev. ed., 1908.
231 Trewin, John C. and Evelyn M. King. *Printer to the House: the story of Hansard.* 1952.
232 Turberville, Arthur S. *The House of Lords in the age of reform, 1784–1837; with an epilogue on aristocracy and the advent of democracy, 1837–1867.* 1958.
233 Wheare, Kenneth C. *The civil service in the constitution.* 1954.
234 White, Brian D. *A history of the corporation of Liverpool, 1835–1914.* Liverpool, 1951.
235 Wilding, Norman W. and Philip Laundy. *An encyclopedia of parliament.* 3rd ed., 1968.
236 Williams, Orlando C. *The clerical organisation of the House of Commons 1661–1850.* Oxford, 1955.
237 —— *The historical development of private bill procedure and standing orders in the House of Commons.* 1948–9, 2 vols.
238 Woodruff, Douglas. *The Tichborne claimant: a Victorian mystery.* 1957. A famous legal case.

4 Biographies

239 Atlay, James B. *The Victorian chancellors.* 1906–8, 2 vols.
240 Benson, Edward F. *Queen Victoria.* 1935.
241 Bolitho, Hector. *Albert: Prince Consort.* 1964.
242 —— *The reign of Queen Victoria.* 1949. An uncritical biography.
243 Coleridge, Ernest H. *Life and correspondence of John Duke Lord Coleridge, Lord Chief Justice of England.* 2 vols., 1904.
244 Eyck, Frank. *The Prince Consort: a political biography.* 1959.
245 Finer, Samuel E. *The life and times of Sir Edwin Chadwick.* 1952.
246 Fulford, Roger. *Queen Victoria.* 1951.
247 Heuston, Robert F. V. *Lives of the Lord Chancellors, 1885–1940.* Oxford, 1964.
248 Hill, Rowland and George B. *The life of Sir Rowland Hill . . . and the history of penny postage.* 1880, 2 vols.
249 Lambert, Royston. *Sir John Simon, 1816–1904, and English social administration.* 1963. A valuable contribution to administrative history.
250 Lee, Sidney. *King Edward VII, I, Birth to accession.* 1925.

251 Lee, Sidney. *Queen Victoria, a biography*. New ed., 1904. The official biography.
252 Longford, Elizabeth, Countess of. *Victoria, R.I.* 1964. American title: *Queen Victoria: born to succeed*. The best biography. See also (1102).
253 Magnus, Philip. *King Edward the Seventh*. 1964.
254 Martin, Theodore. *The life of H.R.H. the Prince Consort*. 1877–80, 5 vols. An official panegyric.
255 O'Brien, Richard Barry. *The life of Lord Russell of Killowen*. 1901.
256 Ponsonby, Arthur. *Henry Ponsonby: Queen Victoria's private secretary*. 1942.
257 Smith, Frank. *The life and work of Sir James Kay-Shuttleworth*. 1923.
258 Stephen, Leslie. *Life of Sir James Fitzjames Stephen*. 1895.
259 Strachey, G. Lytton. *Queen Victoria*. New ed., 1924. Malevolently brilliant.

5 Articles

(See also sec. v, pt. 5, below.)

260 Anderson, Olive. 'Cabinet government and the Crimean war', *EHR*, **79** (July 1964), 548–51.
261 —— 'The Janus face of mid-nineteenth century radicalism: the Administrative Reform Association of 1855', *VS*, **8** (Mar. 1965), 231–42.
262 —— 'The Wensleydale peerage case and the position of the House of Lords in the mid-nineteenth century', *EHR*, **82** (July 1967), 486–502.
263 Blewett, Neal. 'The franchise in the United Kingdom, 1885–1918', *PP*, no. 32 (Dec. 1965), 27–56. See also Grace A. Jones. 'Further thoughts on the franchise', *PP*, no. 34 (July 1966), 134–8.
264 Brand, Jeanne L. 'The parish doctor: England's poor law medical officers and medical reform, 1870–1900', *Bulletin of the History of Medicine*, **35** (Mar.–Apr. 1961), 97–122.
265 Clark, George S. R. Kitson. '"Statesmen in disguise": reflexions on the history of the neutrality of the civil service', *Hist.J.*, **2** (no. 1, 1959), 19–39.
266 Cromwell, Valerie. 'The administrative background to the presentation to parliament of parliamentary papers on foreign affairs in mid-nineteenth century', *Journal of the Society of Archivists*, **2** (Apr. 1963), 302–15.
267 —— 'Interpretations of nineteenth-century administration: an analysis', *VS*, **9** (Mar. 1966), 245–55.
268 Dunbabin, J. P. D. 'Expectations of the new county councils and their realization', *Hist.J.*, **8** (no. 3, 1965), 353–79.
269 Fraser, Peter. 'The growth of ministerial control in the nineteenth-century House of Commons', *EHR*, **75** (July 1960), 444–63.
270 Gosden, P. H. J. H. 'The Board of Education Act, 1899', *British Journal of Educational Studies*, **11** (Nov. 1962), 44–60.
271 Gutchen, Robert M. 'Local governments and centralization in nineteenth-century England', *Hist.J.*, **4** (no. 1, 1961), 85–96.
272 Hart, Jennifer, 'Sir Charles Trevelyan at the Treasury', *EHR*, **75** (Jan. 1960), 92–110.
273 Heuston, Robert F. V. 'Lord Halsbury's judicial appointments', *Law Quarterly Review*, **78** (Oct. 1962), 504–32.
274 Hughes, Edward. 'The changes in parliamentary procedure, 1880–1882', in Richard Pares and Alan J. P. Taylor (eds.). *Essays presented to Sir Lewis Namier*. 1956, pp. 289–319.
275 —— 'Civil service reform', *History*, **27** (June 1942), 51–83.
276 —— 'Sir Charles Trevelyan and civil service reform', *EHR*, **64** (Jan., Apr. 1949), 53–88, 206–34.
277 Lambert, Royston J. 'Central and local relations in mid-Victorian England: the Local Government Act Office, 1858–71', *VS*, **6** (Dec. 1962), 121–50.
278 —— 'A Victorian national health service: state vaccination, 1855–71', *Hist.J.*, **5** (no. 1, 1962), 1–18.
279 MacDonagh, Oliver. 'Coal mines regulation: the first decade. 1842–1852', in *Id. & Inst.*, pp. 58–86.

280 MacDonagh, Oliver. 'Delegated legislation and administrative discretions in the 1850's: a particular study', *VS*, **2** (Sept. 1958), 29–44.

281 —— 'The nineteenth-century revolution in government: a reappraisal', *Hist.J.*, **1** (no. 1, 1958), 52–67. Emphasizes the role of practical experience rather than Benthamite doctrine in the development of administration. Cf. (293).

282 —— 'The regulation of the emigrant traffic from the United Kingdom, 1842–55', *IHS*, **9** (Sept. 1954), 162–89.

283 McDowell, Robert B. 'The Irish courts of law, 1801–1914', *IHS*, **10** (Sept. 1957), 363–91.

284 —— 'The Irish executive in the nineteenth century', *IHS*, **9** (Mar. 1955), 264–80.

285 McGregor, Oliver R. 'Civil servants and the civil service', *Political Quarterly*, **22** (Apr.–June 1951), 154–63.

286 MacLeod, Roy M. 'The Alkali Acts administration 1863–84: the emergence of the civil scientist', *VS*, **9** (Dec. 1965), 85–112.

287 —— 'The frustration of state medicine, 1880–1899', *Medical History*, **11** (Jan. 1967), 15–40.

288 —— 'Government and resource conservation: the Salmon Acts administration, 1860–1886', *JBS*, **7** (May 1968), 144–50.

289 —— 'Medico-legal issues in Victorian medical care', *Medical History*, **10** (Jan. 1966), 44–9.

290 —— 'Social policy and the "floating population": the administration of the Canal Boats Acts 1877–1899', *PP*, **35** (Dec. 1966), 101–32.

291 Manchester, Anthony H. 'The reform of the ecclesiastical courts', *American Journal of Legal History*, **10** (Jan. 1966), 51–75.

292 Midwinter, E. C. 'State intervention at the local level: the new Poor Law in Lancashire', *Hist.J.*, **10** (no. 1, 1967), 106–12.

293 Parris, Henry. 'The nineteenth-century revolution in government: a re-appraisal reappraised', *Hist.J.*, **3** (no. 1, 1960), 17–37. Criticizes (281).

294 —— 'Railway policy in Peel's administration, 1841–1846', *BIHR*, **33** (Nov. 1960), 180–94.

295 Roberts, David. 'How cruel was the Victorian Poor Law?', *Hist.J.*, **6** (no. 1, 1963), 97–107.

296 —— 'Jeremy Bentham and the Victorian administrative state', *VS*, **2** (Mar. 1959), 193–210. De-emphasizes the role of Benthamism.

297 Rose, Michael E. 'The allowance system under the new Poor Law', *EcHR*, 2nd ser., **19** (Dec. 1966), 607–20.

298 Spring, Eileen. 'The settlement of land in nineteenth-century England', *American Journal of Legal History*, **8** (July 1964), 209–23.

299 Stephen, M. D. 'Gladstone and the composition of the final court in ecclesiastical causes, 1850–73', *Hist.J.*, **9** (no. 2, 1966), 191–200.

300 Stuart, C. H. 'The Prince Consort and ministerial politics, 1856–9', in Hugh R. Trevor-Roper (ed.). *Essays in British history presented to Sir Keith Feiling.* 1964, pp. 247–70.

301 Webb, Robert K. 'A Whig inspector', *JMH*, **27** (Dec. 1955), 352–64. Deals with H. S. Tremenheere.

302 Weston, Corinne C. 'The royal mediation in 1884', *EHR*, **82** (Apr. 1967), 296–322.

303 Wilde, Jane H. 'The creation of the marine department of the Board of Trade', *Journal of Transport History*, **2** (Nov. 1956), 193–206.

304 Woodhouse, Margaret K. 'The marriage and divorce bill of 1857', *American Journal of Legal History*, **3** (July 1959), 260–75.

V POLITICAL HISTORY

1 Printed Sources

(See also sec. IV, pt. 1, above.)

305 *The annual register: a review of public events at home and abroad, for the year* . . . *1758–.* Subtitle varies. A rich source.

306 Argyll, Ina E. Campbell, Dowager Duchess of (ed.). *Autobiography and memoirs of the eighth Duke of Argyll.* 1906, 2 vols.

307 Bassett, A. Tilney (ed.). *Gladstone's speeches, descriptive index and bibliography.* 1916. Includes fourteen representative speeches.

308 Beckett, James C. 'Select documents, XXII: Gladstone, Queen Victoria, and the disestablishment of the Irish Church, 1868–9', *IHS,* **13** (Mar. 1962), 38–47.

309 Carty, James (ed.). *Ireland; a documentary record,* II, *Ireland from Grattan's parliament to the great famine, 1783–1850,* III, *Ireland from the great famine to the treaty, 1851–1921.* Dublin, 1951–2.

310 Chamberlain, Joseph. *A political memoir, 1880–92,* ed. Christopher H. D. Howard. 1953.

311 Disraeli, Ralph (ed.). *Lord Beaconsfield's letters, 1830–1852.* 1887. Includes 'Home letters' and 'Correspondence with his sister'.

312 *Dod's parliamentary companion for 1832–.* 1832–. Title varies. Entries for all M.P.s, including statements of political principles and affiliations.

313 Gooch, George P. (ed.). *The later correspondence of Lord John Russell, 1840–1878.* 1925.

314 Grant Duff, Mountstuart E. *Notes from a diary.* 1897–1905, 14 vols. Miscellaneous information, 1851–1901.

315 Greville, Charles C. *The Greville memoirs, 1814–1860,* ed. Lytton Strachey and Roger Fulford. 1938, 8 vols. An outstanding source for political history. This is the complete verbatim edition.

316 Harrison, John F. C. (ed.). *Society and politics in England, 1780–1960: a selection of readings and comments.* New York, 1965.

317 Healy, Timothy M. *Letters and leaders of my day.* 1928, 2 vols. Useful for Irish history.

318 Hewett, Osbert W. (ed.). '. . . *and Mr. Fortescue': a selection from the diaries from 1851 to 1862 of Chichester Fortescue, Lord Carlingford, K.P.* 1958.

319 Hobsbawm, Eric J. (ed.). *Labour's turning point, 1880–1900: extracts from contemporary sources.* 1948.

320 Howard, Christopher H. D. 'Select documents, XXI: Joseph Chamberlain, W. H. O'Shea, and Parnell, 1884, 1891–2', *IHS,* **13** (Mar. 1962), 33–8.

321 Hutchinson, Horace G. (ed.). *Private diaries of the Rt. Hon. Sir Algernon West.* 1922. Gladstone's private secretary, 1892–5.

322 Jennings, Louis L. (ed.). *The Croker papers: the correspondence and diaries of the late Right Honourable John Wilson Croker, Ll.D., F.R.S., Secretary to the Admiralty from 1809 to 1830.* 2nd ed., 1885, 3 vols. Comments on politics from a Tory point of view; also valuable for intellectual history.

323 Kebbel, Thomas E. (ed.). *Selected speeches of the late Right Honourable the Earl of Beaconsfield.* 1882, 2 vols.

324 Kovalev, Y. V. (ed.). *An anthology of chartist literature.* 1957.

325 McCalmont, Frederick H. (ed.). *The parliamentary poll book of all elections from the Reform Act of 1832 to February 1910.* 7th ed., 1910.

326 Maccoby, Simon (ed.). *The English radical tradition, 1763–1914* (The British Political Tradition, bk. 5). 1952.

327 Malmesbury, James Harris, 3rd Earl of. *Memoirs of an ex-minister; an autobiography.* 3rd ed., 1884, 2 vols.

328 Morley, John, Viscount. *Recollections.* 1917, 2 vols.

329 Morris, Max (ed.). *From Cobbett to the chartists, 1815–1848.* 1948.

330 Park, Joseph H. (ed.). *British prime ministers of the nineteenth century; policies and speeches.* New York, 1950.

331 Parker, Charles S. (ed.). *Sir Robert Peel, from his private papers.* 1891–9, 3 vols.
332 *The parliamentary debates.* 3rd ser., 1830–91, 356 vols.; 4th ser., 1892–1908, 199 vols. Also known, until 1891, as *Hansard's parliamentary debates.* The basic source for both houses.
333 Ramm, Agatha (ed.). *The political correspondence of Mr. Gladstone and Lord Granville, 1868–76* (Camden 3rd Series, LXXXI–LXXXII). 1952, 2 vols.
334 —— *The political correspondence of Mr. Gladstone and Lord Granville, 1876–86.* Oxford, 1962, 2 vols.
335 Read, Donald. *Cobden and Bright: a Victorian political partnership.* 1967.
336 *Report of the Special Commission with the evidence and speeches taken verbatim before the judges.* 1896, 12 vols. The Parnell Commission.
337 Saville, John (ed.). *Ernest Jones: chartist.* 1952. Selections from Jones' writings and speeches. Saville's introduction is a scholarly biography.
338 Stockmar, Christian Friedrich, Baron von. *Memoirs of Baron Stockmar,* tr. Georgina A. Müller, ed. F. Max Müller. 1872, 2 vols.
339 Taine, Hippolyte A. *Notes on England,* tr. Edward Hyams. 1957. Notes of a perceptive French visitor in 1858 and 1871.
340 Walling, Robert A. J. (ed.). *The diaries of John Bright.* 1930.
341 Zetland, Lawrence J. L. Dundas, 2nd Marquess of (ed.). *The letters of Disraeli to Lady Chesterfield and Lady Bradford.* 1929, 2 vols.

2 Surveys
(See also sec. III, above.)

342 Beckett, James C. *The making of modern Ireland: 1603–1923.* 1966. The best survey of Irish history.
343 Davis, Henry W. C. *The age of Grey and Peel.* Oxford, 1929.
344 Low, Sidney J. M. and Lloyd C. Sanders. *The history of England during the reign of Victoria (1837–1901)* (The Political History of England, XII). 1907.
345 O'Hegarty, Patrick S. *A history of Ireland under the union, 1801 to 1922.* 1952. Partisan but interesting.
346 Raven, John. *The parliamentary history of England from the passing of the Reform Bill of 1832.* 1885.

3 Monographs
(See also sec. IV, pt. 3, above, and sec. XII, pt. 3, below.)

347 Anderson, Olive. *A liberal state at war: English politics and economics during the Crimean War.* 1967.
348 Arnstein, Walter L. *The Bradlaugh case: a study in late Victorian opinion and politics.* Oxford, 1965. The definitive study.
349 Aspinall, Arthur. *Politics and the press, c. 1780–1850.* 1949.
350 Ausubel, Herman. *In hard times: reformers among the late Victorians.* New York, 1960. An informative study, using exclusively primary sources and emphasizing the 'great depression'.
351 Barnes, Donald G. *A history of the English Corn Laws, 1660–1846.* 1930.
352 Barry, E. Eldon (pseud. of Beatrice F. Grant). *Nationalisation in British politics: the historical background.* 1965.
353 Beales, Hugh L. *The making of social policy.* 1946. A seminal lecture on the development of social legislation and administration.
354 Beer, Max. *A history of British socialism.* 2nd ed., 1940.
355 Brand, Carl F. *British labour's rise to power; eight studies.* 1941.
356 Briggs, Asa (ed.). *Chartist studies.* 1959. A good regional survey.
357 Broderick, John F. *The Holy See and the Irish movement for the repeal of the union with England* (Analecta Gregoriana, 55). Rome, 1951.
358 Brown, Benjamin H. *The tariff reform movement in Great Britain, 1881–1895.* New York, 1943.

359   Brown, Lucy M. *The Board of Trade and the free-trade movement, 1830–1842.*
      Oxford, 1958.
360   Bruce, Maurice. *The coming of the welfare state.* 3rd ed., 1966.
361   Bulmer-Thomas, Ivor. *The growth of the British party system,* I, *1640–1923.*
      1965.
362   Bünger, Siegfried. *Friedrich Engels und die Britische sozialistische Bewegung,
      1881–1895.* Berlin, 1962.
363   Buxton, Sydney C., 1st Earl. *Finance and politics, an historical study, 1783–
      1885.* 1888, 2 vols.
364   Cheyney, Edward P. *Modern English reform, from individualism to socialism.*
      1931.
365   Clark, George S. R. Kitson. *Peel and the Conservative party: a study in party
      politics, 1832–1841.* 2nd ed., 1964.
366   Clarkson, J. Dunsmore. *Labour and nationalism in Ireland.* New York, 1925.
367   Clayton, Joseph. *The rise and decline of socialism in Great Britain, 1884–1924.*
      1926.
368   Cole, George D. H. *British working-class politics, 1832–1914.* 1941. One of
      the basic works in the field, written from a Fabian point of view.
369   —— *Chartist portraits.* 2nd ed., 1965.
370   Cole, Margaret I. *The story of Fabian socialism.* 1961.
371   Collins, Henry and Chimen Abramsky. *Karl Marx and the British labour
      movement: years of the first International.* 1965.
372   Conacher, James B. *The Aberdeen coalition, 1852–55: a study in mid-nineteenth-
      century party politics.* Cambridge, 1968.
373   Costigan, Giovanni. *Makers of modern England: the force of individual genius
      in history.* New York, 1966. Includes essays on J. S. Mill, Newman,
      Gladstone, Disraeli and the Webbs.
374   Cowherd, Raymond G. *The humanitarians and the ten hour movement in
      England.* Boston, 1956. A brief pamphlet with bibliographic appendix.
375   —— *The politics of English dissent; the religious aspects of liberal and
      humanitarian reform movements from 1815 to 1848.* 1959.
376   Cowling, Maurice. *1867: Disraeli, Gladstone and revolution: the passing of the
      second Reform Bill.* 1967.
377   Crook, David P. *American democracy in English politics, 1815–1850.* Oxford,
      1965.
378   Curtis, Lewis P., Jr. *Coercion and conciliation in Ireland, 1880–1892: a study
      in Conservative unionism.* Princeton, 1963. A useful contribution.
379   Derry, John W. *The radical tradition: Tom Paine to Lloyd George.* 1967.
      Essays in political thought.
380   Dolléans, Edouard. *Le chartisme.* Paris, 1912–13, 2 vols.
381   —— *Histoire du mouvement ouvrier.* Paris, 1936–53, 3 vols.
382   Elton, Godfrey, Baron. *'England arise !' a study of the pioneering days of the
      labour movement.* 1931.
383   Fussell, George E. *From Tolpuddle to T.U.C.: a century of farm labourers'
      politics.* Slough, 1948.
384   Gash, Norman. *Politics in the age of Peel, a study in the technique of parlia-
      mentary representation, 1830–1850.* 1953. The major contribution of the
      leading political historian of the period, a close analysis of political practices.
385   —— *Reaction and reconstruction in English politics 1832–1852.* Oxford, 1965.
      The Ford Lectures for 1964, a general and synoptic examination of the
      practical adjustment of politics to reform.
386   Gillespie, Frances E. *Labor and politics in England, 1850–1867.* Durham,
      N.C., 1927.
387   Glasier, John B. *William Morris and the early days of the socialist movement;
      being reminiscences of Morris' work as a propagandist, and observations on his
      character and genius, with some account of the persons and circumstances of the
      early socialist agitation . . .* 1921. Includes letters.
388   Gorst, Harold E. *The fourth party.* 1906.
389   Guedalla, Philip. *Gladstone and Palmerston.* 1928. Contains useful cor-
      respondence.
390   Guttsman, William L. *The British political elite, 1832–1935.* 1963.

391 Gwyn, William B. *Democracy and the cost of politics in Britain.* 1962.
392 Gwynn, Denis. *O'Connell, Davis, and the Colleges Bill.* Cork, 1948. The controversy over Peel's educational scheme for Ireland.
393 —— *Young Ireland and 1848.* Cork, 1949.
394 Hammond, John L. *Gladstone and the Irish nation.* 2nd ed., 1964.
395 Hammond, John L. and Michael R. D. Foot. *Gladstone and liberalism.* 1952.
396 Hanham, Harold J. *Elections and party management: politics in the time of Disraeli and Gladstone.* 1959. An important, detailed analysis of political organization, 1868–85.
397 Harrison, Royden J. *Before the socialists; studies in labour and politics, 1861–1881.* 1965.
398 Hearnshaw, Fossey J. C. *Conservatism in England, an analytical, historical and political survey.* 1932.
399 Hill, Richard L. *Toryism and the people, 1832–1846.* 1929.
400 Hovell, Mark. *The chartist movement.* 3rd ed., Manchester, 1966. A posthumous work, originally published 1918, this remains the best single book on the subject.
401 Humphrey, Arthur W. *A history of labour representation.* 1912.
402 Hurst, Michael C. *Joseph Chamberlain and Liberal reunion: the round table conference of 1887.* 1967.
403 —— *Joseph Chamberlain and west Midland politics, 1886–1895* (Dugdale Society Occasional Papers, no. 15). Oxford, 1962.
404 Jennings, William Ivor. *Party politics, I, Appeal to the people, II, The growth of parties, III, The stuff of politics.* Cambridge, 1962, 3 vols.
405 Lampson, G. Locker. *A consideration of the state of Ireland in the nineteenth century.* 1907.
406 Lee, Henry W. *Social-democracy in Britain. Fifty years of the socialist movement,* ed. Herbert Tracey. 1935. Not scholarly, but still useful on the Social Democratic Federation.
407 Lynd, Helen M. *England in the eighteen-eighties: toward a social basis for freedom.* New York, 1945.
408 Lyons, Francis S. L. *The fall of Parnell, 1890–91.* 1960. An excellent narrative, meticulously researched.
409 —— *The Irish parliamentary party* (Studies in Irish History, IV). 1951. A study of the inner workings of the party.
410 MacBriar, Alan M. *Fabian socialism and English politics 1884–1918.* Cambridge, 1962.
411 McCaffrey, Lawrence J. *Daniel O'Connell and the repeal year.* Lexington, Ky., 1966.
412 —— *Irish federalism in the 1870's: a study in conservative nationalism* (Transactions of the American Philosophical Society, new ser., LII). Philadelphia, 1962. A good study of Isaac Butt's movement.
413 —— *The Irish question, 1800–1922.* Lexington, Ky., 1968.
414 McCallum, Ronald B. *The Liberal party from Earl Grey to Asquith.* 1963.
415 Maccoby, Simon. *English radicalism, III, 1832–1852, IV, 1853–1886, V, 1886–1914.* 1935–53, 3 vols. A detailed and magisterial study.
416 McCord, Norman. *The Anti-Corn Law League, 1838–1846.* 1958. The fullest account.
417 McDowell, Robert B. *British conservatism, 1832–1914.* 1959.
418 —— *Public opinion and government policy in Ireland, 1801–1846* (Studies in Irish History, V). 1952. A useful guide to politics and society.
419 Mansergh, Nicholas. *Britain and Ireland.* Rev. ed., 1946.
420 —— *The Irish question, 1840–1921.* New ed., 1965. Originally entitled *Ireland in the age of reform and revolution.* 1940. An impartial and original study of the national question.
421 Marshall, Leon S. *The development of public opinion in Manchester.* Syracuse, N.Y., 1946.
422 Martin, B. Kingsley. *The triumph of Lord Palmerston, a study of public opinion in England before the Crimean war.* 1924.
423 Mather, Frederick C. *Public order in the age of the chartists.* Manchester, 1959. Useful on the development of police forces.

424 Mills, J. Travis. *John Bright and the Quakers*. 1935, 2 vols.
425 Moody, Theodore W. and James C. Beckett (eds.). *Ulster since 1800: a political and economic survey*. 1954. Twelve radio lectures.
426 Morgan, Kenneth O. *Wales in British politics, 1868–1922*. Cardiff, 1963.
427 Morris, Homer L. *Parliamentary franchise reform in England from 1885 to 1918*. New York, 1921.
428 Morton, Arthur L. and George Tate. *The British labour movement, 1770–1920: a history*. 1956.
429 Nowlan, Kevin B. *The politics of repeal: a study in the relations between Great Britain and Ireland, 1841–50*. 1965.
430 O'Brien, Conor Cruise. *Parnell and his party, 1880–1890*. 2nd ed., Oxford, 1964. The classic study, brilliant and original.
431 O'Brien, Conor Cruise (ed.). *The shaping of modern Ireland*. 1960. Biographical essays, 1891–1916.
432 O'Leary, Cornelius. *The elimination of corrupt practices in British elections, 1868–1911*. Oxford, 1962.
433 Ostrogorskii, Moisei I. *Democracy and the organization of political parties*, tr. Frederick Clarke. 1902, 2 vols.
434 Palmer, Norman D. *The Irish Land League crisis*. New Haven, 1940.
435 Park, Joseph H. *The English reform bill of 1867*. New York, 1920. Rather thin; see (376) and (454).
436 Patterson, A. Temple. *Radical Leicester: the history of Leicester, 1780–1850*. Leicester, 1954. Useful for social as well as political history.
437 Pelling, Henry. *The origins of the Labour party, 1880–1900*. 2nd ed., Oxford, 1965. A major contribution, with a useful bibliography.
438 —— *Social geography of British elections, 1885–1910*. 1967.
439 Pike, E. Royston. *Pioneers of social change*. 1963. Includes chapters on Chadwick, Shaftesbury and Mill.
440 Poirier, Philip P. *The advent of the British Labour party*. 1958.
441 Pomfret, John E. *The struggle for land in Ireland, 1800–1923*. Princeton, 1930.
442 Reid, J. H. Stewart. *The origins of the British Labour party*. Minneapolis, 1955.
443 Robb, Janet H. *The Primrose League, 1883–1906*. 1942.
444 Rover, Constance. *Women's suffrage and party politics in Britain, 1866–1914*. Toronto, 1967.
445 Ryan, Desmond. *The phoenix flame: a study of Fenianism and John Devoy*. 1937.
446 Sanders, William S. *Early socialist days*. 1927.
447 Saville, John (ed.). *Democracy and the labour movement*. 1954. A Marxist symposium.
448 Schuyler, Robert L. *The fall of the old colonial system: a study in British free trade, 1770–1870*. New York, 1945.
449 Semmel, Bernard. *The Governor Eyre controversy*. 1962.
450 —— *Imperialism and social reform: English social-imperial thought, 1895–1914*. 1960.
451 Seymour, Charles. *Electoral reform in England and Wales: the development and operation of the parliamentary franchise, 1832–1885*. New Haven, 1915.
452 Shannon, Richard T. *Gladstone and the Bulgarian agitation, 1876*. 1963.
453 Slesser, Henry H. *History of the Liberal party*. 1944.
454 Smith, Francis B. *The making of the second Reform Bill*. Cambridge, 1966.
455 Smith, Paul. *Disraelian conservatism and social reform*. 1967.
456 Southgate, Donald. *The passing of the Whigs, 1832–1886*. 1962.
457 Stansky, Peter. *Ambitions and strategies: the struggle for the leadership of the Liberal party in the 1890's*. Oxford, 1964. An interesting account of party quarrels, 1894–8.
458 Strachey, Rachel C. *'The cause'; a short history of the women's movement in Great Britain*. 1928.
459 Strauss, Eric. *Irish nationalism and British democracy*. 1951.
460 Taylor, Ernest R. *Methodism and politics 1791–1851*. Cambridge, 1935.
461 Thompson, Paul. *Socialists, Liberals and Labour: the struggle for London, 1885–1914*. Toronto, 1967.

462 Thornton, Archibald P. *The imperial idea and its enemies: a study in British power.* 1959. A brilliant study of the attitudes of the ruling classes.

463 Tuchman, Barbara. *The proud tower: a portrait of the world before the war, 1890–1914.* New York, 1965. The first chapter is a fascinating account of the government of 1895–1902.

464 Vincent, John R. *The formation of the Liberal party, 1857–1868.* 1966.

465 —— *Pollbooks: how Victorians voted.* Cambridge, 1967. Collates and interprets pollbooks for 130 elections, 1826–72, with statistical tables.

466 Ward, John T. *The factory movement, 1830–1855.* 1962.

467 Watson, Robert S. *The National Liberal Federation from its commencement to the general election of 1906.* 1907.

468 Whyte, John H. *The independent Irish party, 1850–9.* Oxford, 1958. Rediscovers an almost forgotten third party.

469 —— *The Tenant League and Irish politics in the eighteen fifties.* Dundalk, 1963. A short study.

470 Williams, David. *John Frost: a study in chartism.* Cardiff, 1939. An excellent study of Welsh chartism and the Newport riots of 1839.

471 —— *The Rebecca riots: a study in agrarian discontent.* Cardiff, 1955. The anti-tollbooth riots of the 1840s.

472 Williams, Glanmor (ed.). *Merthyr politics: the making of a working-class tradition.* Cardiff, 1966.

473 Williams, William Evan. *The rise of Gladstone to the leadership of the Liberal party, 1859 to 1868.* Cambridge, 1934.

474 Witmer, Helen E. *The property qualifications of members of parliament.* 1943. The background of repeal in 1858.

475 Wright, Leslie C. *Scottish chartism.* Edinburgh, 1963.

4 Biographies

(See also sec. IV, pt. 4, above.)

476 Abels, Jules. *The Parnell tragedy.* 1966.

477 Armytage, Walter H. G. *A. J. Mundella, 1825–1897: the Liberal background to the labour movement.* 1951.

478 Ashley, Anthony Evelyn M. *The life and correspondence of Henry John Temple, Viscount Palmerston.* 1879, 2 vols. Inadequate and outdated, but contains some documentation.

479 Ausubel, Herman. *John Bright, Victorian reformer.* New York, 1966. See also (563).

480 Balfour, Lady Frances. *The life of George, 4th Earl of Aberdeen, K.G., K.T.* 1923, 2 vols.

481 Bell, Herbert C. F. *Lord Palmerston.* 1936, 2 vols. The standard biography. See also (556).

482 Best, Geoffrey F. A. *Shaftesbury.* 1964.

483 Blake, Robert. *Disraeli.* 1966. One of the masterpieces of the biographical art; supersedes all earlier one-volume lives of Disraeli.

484 Bonner, Hypatia B. and John M. Robertson. *Charles Bradlaugh: a record of his life and work.* 1894. Partisan.

485 Brightfield, Myron F. *John Wilson Croker.* Berkeley, 1940.

486 Bryce, James, Viscount. *Studies in contemporary biography.* 1927. Sketches of Disraeli, A. P. Stanley, T. H. Green, Tait, Trollope, J. R. Green, Jessel, Cairns, James Fraser, Northcote, Parnell, Manning, Freeman, Lowe, Robertson Smith, Sidgwick, E. E. Bowen, Godkin, Acton and Gladstone.

487 Cecil, Lord David. *Lord M.: the later life of Lord Melbourne.* 1954. Reissued, with earlier material, as *Melbourne.* 1965. Delightful reading, stronger on the personal than the political side.

488 Cecil, Lady Gwendolyn. *Life of Robert, Marquess of Salisbury.* 1921–32, 4 vols.

489 Childers, Edmund S. E. *The life and correspondence of the Rt. Hon. Hugh C. E. Childers, 1827–1896.* 1901, 2 vols.

17

490 Chilston, Eric A. Akers-Douglas, 3rd Viscount. *Chief whip: the political life and times of Aretas Akers-Douglas, 1st Viscount Chilston.* 1961. A good life of a significant lesser figure.
491 —— *W. H. Smith.* 1965.
492 Churchill, Winston L. S. *Lord Randolph Churchill.* Rev. ed., 1952. Interesting because of its author.
493 Clark, George S. R. Kitson. *Peel* (Great Lives Series, LXXV). 1936.
494 Crewe, Robert O. A. Crewe-Milnes, Marquess of. *Lord Rosebery.* 1931, 2 vols.
495 Driver, Cecil H. *Tory radical: the life of Richard Oastler.* New York, 1946.
496 Dugdale, Blanche E. C. *Arthur James Balfour,* I. 1936.
497 Elletson, Daniel H. *The Chamberlains.* 1966.
498 Elliot, Arthur R. D. *The life of George Joachim Goschen.* 1911.
499 Erickson, Arvel B. *Edward T. Cardwell: Peelite* (Transactions of the American Philosophical Society, new ser., XLIX, pt. 2). Philadelphia, 1959.
500 —— *The public career of Sir James Graham.* Oxford, 1952.
501 Eyck, Erich. *Gladstone,* tr. Bernard Miall. 1938.
502 Fowler, William S. *A study in radicalism and dissent; the life and times of Henry Joseph Wilson, 1833–1914.* 1961.
503 Fraser, Peter. *Joseph Chamberlain: radicalism and empire, 1868–1914.* 1966.
504 Gardiner, Alfred G. *The life of Sir William Harcourt.* 1923, 2 vols.
505 —— *Sir John Benn and the progressive movement.* 1925.
506 Garvin, James L. *Life of Joseph Chamberlain,* completed by Julian Amery. 1932–51, 4 vols.
507 Gathorne-Hardy, Alfred E. *Gathorne Hardy, first Earl of Cranbrook, a memoir with extracts from his diary and correspondence.* 1910, 2 vols.
508 Gladstone, Herbert J., Viscount. *After thirty years.* 1928. A reminiscence of W. E. Gladstone by his son.
509 Gollin, Alfred M. *Proconsul in politics: a study of Lord Milner in opposition and in power, 1854–1905.* 1964.
510 Guedalla, Philip. *Palmerston, 1784–1865.* 1927.
511 Gwynn, Denis R. *Daniel O'Connell, the Irish liberator.* Rev. ed., Cork and Oxford, 1947.
512 Gwynn, Stephen and Gertrude M. Tuckwell. *Life of the Right Hon. Sir Charles W. Dilke.* 1917, 2 vols.
513 Hammond, John L. and Barbara. *James Stansfeld: a Victorian champion of sex equality.* 1932.
514 —— *Lord Shaftesbury.* 4th ed., 1936. See also (482).
515 Hardinge, Arthur H. *The life of Henry Edward Molyneux Herbert, fourth Earl of Carnarvon, 1831–1890,* ed. Elisabeth, Countess of Carnarvon. 1925, 3 vols.
516 Hicks-Beach, Lady Victoria A. *Life of Sir Michael Hicks-Beach (Earl St. Aldwyn).* 1932, 2 vols.
517 Hobson, John A. *Richard Cobden, the international man.* 1919.
518 Hodder, Edwin. *The life and work of the seventh Earl of Shaftesbury.* 1886, 3 vols.
519 Holland, Bernard H. *The life of Spencer Compton, eighth Duke of Devonshire.* 1911, 2 vols.
520 Hughes, Emrys. *Keir Hardie.* 1950.
521 James, Robert R. *Lord Randolph Churchill.* 1959. The most competent biography.
522 —— *Rosebery.* 1963.
523 Jenkins, Roy. *Asquith.* 1964. A good biography by a potential successor.
524 —— *Sir Charles Dilke: a Victorian tragedy.* 1958.
525 Johnson, Leonard G. *General T. Perronet Thompson, 1783–1869; his military, literary and political campaigns.* 1957.
526 Jones, Wilbur D. *Lord Derby and Victorian conservatism.* Oxford, 1956.
527 Kennedy, Aubrey L. *Salisbury, 1830–1903: portrait of a statesman.* 1953. Presents a good broad picture.
528 Lang, Andrew. *Life, letters and diaries of Sir Stafford Northcote, first Earl of Iddesleigh.* New ed., Edinburgh, 1891.

529 Leader, Robert E. *Life and letters of John Arthur Roebuck, P.C., Q.C., M.P.* 1897. Needs to be superseded.
530 Lyons, Francis S. L. *Parnell*. Dundalk, 1963. A short life.
531 Macintyre, Angus. *The liberator: Daniel O'Connell and the Irish party, 1830–1847.* 1965.
532 Magnus, Philip M. *Gladstone: a biography*. 1954. This distinguished and delightful book is the best biography. See also (1088).
533 Martin, Arthur P. *Life and letters of the Rt. Hon. Robert Lowe, Viscount Sherbrooke.* 1893, 2 vols. Old-fashioned, but has useful materials.
534 Maurois, André. *Disraeli; a picture of the Victorian age*, tr. Hamish Miles. 1927. Distinguished as literature, not history.
535 Maxwell, Herbert E. *Life and letters of George William Frederick, fourth Earl of Clarendon.* 1913, 2 vols.
536 Monypenny, William F. and George E. Buckle. *The life of Benjamin Disraeli, Earl of Beaconsfield.* 1910–20, 6 vols. 2nd ed., 1929, 2 vols. Still a major source for information.
537 Moody, Theodore W. *Thomas Davis, 1814–1845.* Dublin, 1945. Useful for Young Ireland.
538 Morley, John. *Life of Richard Cobden.* 1913, 2 vols.
539 —— *The life of William Ewart Gladstone.* 1903, 3 vols. A biographical classic, still valuable because of the author's personal knowledge of his subject.
540 Munford, William A. *William Ewart, M.P., 1798–1869: portrait of a radical.* 1960.
541 O'Brien, R. Barry. *Life of Charles Stewart Parnell.* 1898–9, 2 vols.
542 Parker, Charles S. *Life and letters of Sir James Graham, second baronet of Netherby, P.C., G.C.B., 1792–1861.* 1907, 2 vols. Superseded by (566).
543 Pearson, Hesketh. *Labby (the life and character of Henry Labouchere).* 1936.
544 Pope-Hennessy, James. *Monckton-Milnes: the flight of youth, 1851–1885.* 1951.
545 —— *Monckton-Milnes: the years of promise, 1809–1851.* 1949. A graceful life of a graceful failure; useful also for intellectual history.
546 Ramsay, Anna A. W. *Sir Robert Peel.* 1928. Will be superseded when Gash's biography is completed.
547 Read, Donald and Eric Glasgow. *Feargus O'Connor, Irishman and chartist.* 1961.
548 Reid, Thomas Wemyss. *Life of the Right Honourable William Edward Forster.* 1888, 2 vols.
549 Roth, Cecil. *Benjamin Disraeli, Earl of Beaconsfield.* New York, 1952. Useful primarily for the Jewish aspects.
550 Rowse, Alfred L. *The later Churchills.* 1958.
551 Ryan, Desmond. *The Fenian chief.* Dublin, 1967. A biography of James Stephens.
552 Saintsbury, George. *The Earl of Derby.* 1892. A short essay; must be supplemented by (526).
553 Schoyen, Albert R. *The chartist challenge: a portrait of George Julian Harney.* New York, 1958.
554 Sheehy-Skeffington, Francis. *Michael Davitt, revolutionary, agitator and labour leader.* 2nd ed., 1967.
555 Somervell, David C. *Disraeli and Gladstone; a duo-biographical sketch.* 1925.
556 Southgate, Donald. *'The most English minister . . .': the policies and politics of Palmerston.* 1966.
557 Spender, John A. *The life of the Right Hon. Sir Henry Campbell-Bannerman, G.C.B.* 1923, 2 vols.
558 Spender, John A. and Cyril Asquith. *Life of Herbert Henry Asquith, Lord Oxford and Asquith,* I. 1932.
559 Stanmore, Arthur Hamilton-Gordon, 1st Baron. *Sidney Herbert, Lord Herbert of Lea; a memoir.* 1906, 2 vols.
560 Stewart, William. *J. Keir Hardie.* 1921.
561 Thornley, David. *Isaac Butt and home rule.* 1964.
562 Tierney, Michael (ed.). *Daniel O'Connell, nine centenary essays.* Dublin, 1949.
563 Trevelyan, George M. *The life of John Bright.* 1913.
564 —— *Sir George Otto Trevelyan: a memoir.* 1932.

565 Walpole, Spencer. *The life of Lord John Russell*. 1889, 2 vols.
566 Ward, John T. *Sir James Graham*. 1967.
567 Whibley, Charles. *Lord John Manners and his friends*. 1925, 2 vols.
568 White, Terence de Vere. *The road of excess*. Dublin, 1946. Despite the title, this is a sympathetic biography of Isaac Butt. Limited scholarly apparatus.
569 Wolf, Lucien. *Life of the first Marquess of Ripon*. 1921, 2 vols.
570 Young, Kenneth. *Arthur James Balfour: the happy life of the politician, prime minister, statesman and philosopher, 1848–1930*. 1963.

5 Articles
(See also sec. IV, pt. 5, above, and sec. XII, pt. 5, below.)

571 Altholz, Josef L. 'The political behavior of the English Catholics, 1850–67', *JBS*, **3** (Nov. 1964), 89–103.
572 Altick, Richard D. '"Our gallant colonel" in *Punch* and parliament', *Bulletin of the New York Public Library*, **69** (Sept. 1965), 424–45. On the ineffable Col. Sibthorp.
573 Armytage, Walter H. G. 'The railway rates question and the fall of the third Gladstone ministry', *EHR*, **65** (Jan. 1950), 18–51. See (730).
574 Arnstein, Walter L. 'Gladstone and the Bradlaugh case', *VS*, **5** (June 1962), 303–30.
575 —— 'Parnell and the Bradlaugh case', *IHS*, **13** (Mar. 1963), 212–35.
576 Auchmuty, James J. 'Acton's election as an Irish member of parliament', *EHR*, **61** (Sept. 1946), 394–405. A delightful sketch of the Carlow election, 1859.
577 Aydelotte, William O. 'The conservative and radical interpretations of early Victorian social legislation', *VS*, **11** (Dec. 1967), 225–36. A computer study finding no relation between conservatism or radicalism and voting on social legislation.
578 —— 'The country gentlemen and the repeal of the Corn Laws', *EHR*, **82** (Jan. 1967), 47–60.
579 —— 'The House of Commons in the 1840's', *History*, **39** (Oct. 1954), 249–62.
580 —— 'Parties and issues in early Victorian England', *JBS*, **5** (May 1966), 95–114. An important computer-based study of parliamentary voting.
581 —— 'Voting patterns in the British House of Commons in the 1840s', *Comparative Studies in Society and History*, **5** (Jan. 1963), 134–63. The pioneering work in computer studies of Victorian politics.
582 Bagwell, Philip D. 'The railway interest: its organisation and influence, 1839–1914', *Journal of Transport History*, **7** (Nov. 1965), 65–86.
583 Beales, Derek E. D. 'Parliamentary parties and the "independent" member, 1810–1860', in *Id. & Inst.*, pp. 1–19.
584 Bedarida, François. 'Une crise de la conscience nationale en 1886. L'Angleterre en face de l'autonomie de l'Irlande', *Revue française de science politique*, **8** (Juin 1958), 277–310.
585 Bell, Aldon D. 'Administration and finance of the Reform League, 1865–1867', *IRSH*, **10** (pt. 3, 1965), 385–409.
586 Bell, Herbert C. 'Palmerston and parliamentary representation', *JMH*, **4** (June 1932), 186–213.
587 Blake, Robert. 'The rise of Disraeli', in Hugh R. Trevor-Roper (ed.). *Essays in British history presented to Sir Keith Feiling*. 1964, pp. 219–46.
588 Brebner, John Bartlet. 'Laissez-faire and state intervention in nineteenth-century Britain', *JEcH*, **8** (Supplement, 1948), 59–73. Reprinted in *Ess. Ec. Hist.*, III, 252–62. Emphasizes the role of Benthamism.
589 Briggs, Asa. 'Middle-class consciousness in English politics, 1780–1846', *PP*, **9** (Apr. 1956), 65–74.
590 —— 'Social structure and politics in Birmingham and Lyons (1825–1848)', *British Journal of Sociology*, **1** (Mar. 1950), 67–80.
591 —— 'The welfare state in historical perspective', *Archives européennes de sociologie*, **2** (no. 2, 1961), 221–58.

592 Burn, William L. 'Free trade in land: an aspect of the Irish question', *TRHS*, 4th ser., **31** (1949), 61–74. On the Encumbered Estates Act.

593 Butler, James R. M. 'Imperial questions in British politics, 1868–1880', in *CHBE*, III, 17–64.

594 Cahill, Gilbert A. 'Irish Catholicism and English toryism', *Review of Politics*, **19** (Jan. 1957), 62–76. On the political uses of the no-Popery issue.

595 Calkins, Wendell N. 'A Victorian free trade lobby', *EcHR*, 2nd ser., **13** (Aug. 1960), 90–104. On the Liverpool Financial Reform Association.

596 Checkland, Sydney G. 'The mind of the City, 1870–1914', *Oxford Economic Papers*, **9** (Oct. 1957), 261–78. On the influence of London on the government.

597 Chilston, Eric A. Akers-Douglas, 3rd Viscount. 'The 1880 election: a historical landmark', *Parliamentary Affairs*, **14** (Autumn 1961), 477–93.

598 —— 'The Tories and Parnell, 1885–1891', *Parliamentary Affairs*, **14** (Winter 1960–1), 55–71.

599 Clapham, John H. 'Great Britain and free trade (1841–52)', in *CMH*, XI, 1–21.

600 Clark, George S. R. Kitson. 'The electorate and the repeal of the Corn Laws', *TRHS*, 5th ser., **1** (1951), 109–126.

601 —— 'Hunger and politics in 1842', *JMH*, **25** (Dec. 1953), 355–74.

602 —— 'The repeal of the Corn Laws and the politics of the forties', *EcHR*, 2nd ser., **4** (no. 1, 1951), 1–13.

603 Clarke, Randall. 'The relations between O'Connell and the Young Irelanders', *IHS*, **3** (Mar. 1942), 18–30.

604 Cole, Margaret I. 'The Fabian Society', *Political Quarterly*, **15** (July–Sept. 1944), 245–56.

605 Collieu, E. G. 'Lord Brougham and the Conservatives', in Hugh R. Trevor-Roper (ed.). *Essays in British history presented to Sir Keith Feiling*. 1964, pp. 195–218.

606 Coltham, Stephen. 'George Potter, the Junta, and the *Bee-Hive*', *IRSH*, **9** (pt. 3, 1964), 391–432; **10** (pt. 1, 1965), 23–65.

607 Conacher, James B. 'Mr. Gladstone seeks a seat', *Canadian Historical Association. Report of the Annual Meeting* (1962), 55–67. Covers 1845–7.

608 —— 'Peel and the Peelites, 1846–1850', *EHR*, **73** (July 1958), 431–52.

609 Corish, Patrick J. 'Cardinal Cullen and the National Association of Ireland', *Reportorium Novum*, **3** (no. 1, 1961–2), 13–61.

610 Cornford, James P. 'The parliamentary foundations of the Hotel Cecil', in *Id. & Inst.*, pp. 268–311.

611 —— 'The transformation of Conservatism in the late nineteenth century', *VS*, **7** (Sept. 1963), 35–66. A computer-based study of the effects of population shifts and single-member constituencies.

612 Cowling, Maurice. 'Disraeli, Derby and fusion, October 1865 to July 1866', *Hist.J.*, **8** (no. 1, 1965), 31–71.

613 Crapster, Basil L. 'Scotland and the Conservative party in 1876', *JMH*, **29** (Dec. 1957), 355–60.

614 Crowley, Desmond W. 'The "crofters' party", 1885–1892', *SHR*, **35** (Oct. 1956), 110–26.

615 Dreyer, F. A. 'The Whigs and the political crisis of 1845', *EHR*, **80** (July 1965), 514–37.

616 Duffy, Albert E. P. 'Differing policies and personality rivalries in the origins of the Independent Labour Party', *VS*, **6** (Sept. 1962), 43–65. The personalities are Mann, Champion, Keir Hardie, Shaw and Blatchford.

617 Dunbabin, John P. D. 'Parliamentary elections in Great Britain 1868–1900: a psephological note', *EHR*, **81** (Jan. 1966), 82–99.

618 —— 'The politics of the establishment of county councils', *Hist.J.*, **6** (no. 2, 1963), 226–52.

619 Dunlop, Robert. 'Ireland and the home rule movement', in *CMH*, XII, 65–90.

620 Ensor, Robert C. K. 'Some political and economic interactions in later Victorian England', *TRHS*, 4th ser., **31** (1949), 17–28. On the Irish issue as a factor in the rise of Conservatism among the propertied classes.

621 Fay, Charles R. 'The movement towards free trade, 1820–1853', in *CHBE*, II, 388–414.

622 Feuchtwanger, E. J. 'The Conservative party under the impact of the second Reform Act', *VS*, 2 (June 1959), 289–304.

623 —— 'J. E. Gorst and the central organisation of the Conservative party', *BIHR*, 32 (Nov. 1959), 192–208.

624 Fraser, Peter. 'The Liberal Unionist alliance: Chamberlain, Hartington, and the Conservatives, 1886–1904', *EHR*, 77 (Jan. 1962), 53–75.

625 Gallagher, John and Ronald Robinson. 'The imperialism of free trade', *EHR*, 2nd ser., 6 (Aug. 1953), 1–15. A revision of the concepts of mid-Victorian policy. See their *Africa and the Victorians: the official mind of imperialism*. 1961.

626 Gash, Norman. 'F. R. Bonham: Conservative "political secretary"', 1832–47', *EHR*, 63 (Oct. 1948), 502–22.

627 —— 'Peel and the party system, 1830–1850', *TRHS*, 5th ser., 1 (1951), 47–69.

628 Glaser, John F. 'English nonconformity and the decline of Liberalism', *AHR*, 63 (Jan. 1958), 352–63. Relates the decline of the nonconformist ethic to politics.

629 —— 'Parnell's fall and the non-conformist conscience', *IHS*, 12 (Sept. 1960), 119–38.

630 Golby, John. 'A great electioneer and his motives: the fourth Duke of Newcastle', *Hist.J.*, 8 (no. 2, 1965), 201–18.

631 Gooch, George P. 'Great Britain and Ireland (1832–41)', in *CMH*, X, 655–84.

632 Goodman, Gordon L. 'Liberal Unionism: the revolt of the Whigs', *VS*, 3 (Dec. 1959), 173–89.

633 Gossman, Norbert J. 'Republicanism in nineteenth century England', *IRSH*, 7 (pt. 1, 1962), 47–60.

634 Guttsman, William L. 'The changing social structure of the British political elite, 1886–1935', *British Journal of Sociology*, 2 (Apr. 1951), 122–34.

635 Hanham, Harold J. 'British party finance, 1868–1880', *BIHR*, 27 (May 1954), 69–90.

636 —— 'Mid-century Scottish nationalism: romantic and radical', in *Id. & Inst.*, pp. 143–79.

637 —— 'The sale of honours in late Victorian England', *VS*, 3 (Mar. 1960), 277–89.

638 Harnetty, Peter. 'The imperialism of free trade: Lancashire, India, and the cotton supply question', *JBS*, 6 (Nov. 1966), 70–96.

639 —— 'The Indian cotton duties controversy, 1894–1896', *EHR*, 77 (Oct. 1962), 684–702.

640 Harrison, Brian. 'The Sunday trading riots of 1855', *Hist.J.*, 8 (no. 2, 1965), 219–45.

641 Harrison, Brian and Patricia Hollis. 'Chartism, Liberalism and the life of Robert Lowery', *EHR*, 82 (July 1967), 503–35.

642 Harrison, Henry. 'Parnell's vindication', *IHS*, 5 (Mar. 1947), 231–43.

643 Harrison, Royden. 'The British working class and the general election of 1868', *IRSH*, 5 (pt. 3, 1960), 424–55; 6 (pt. 1, 1961), 74–109.

644 —— 'The 10th April of Spencer Walpole: the problem of revolution in relation to reform, 1865–1867', *IRSH*, 7 (pt. 3, 1962), 351–99. On the Hyde Park riots of 1865.

645 Hart, Jennifer. 'Nineteenth-century social reform: a Tory interpretation of history', *PP*, 31 (July 1965), 39–61. Stresses the influence of Benthamite political ideas.

646 Hennock, E. P. 'Finance and politics in urban local government in England, 1835–1900', *Hist.J.*, 6 (no. 2, 1963), 212–25.

647 Hernon, Joseph M., Jr. 'The use of the American civil war in the debate over Irish home rule', *AHR*, 69 (July 1964), 1022–6.

648 Herrick, Francis H. 'Gladstone, Newman, and Ireland in 1851', *Catholic Historical Review*, 47 (Oct. 1961), 342–50.

649 —— 'The origins of the National Liberal Federation', *JMH*, 17 (June 1945), 116–29.

650 Herrick, Francis H. 'The second reform movement in England', *JHI*, 9 (Apr. 1948), 174–92.

651 Himmelfarb, Gertrude. 'The politics of democracy: the English Reform Act of 1867', *JBS*, 6 (Nov. 1966), 97–138. A perversely brilliant neo-conservative analysis.

652 Howard, Christopher H. D. 'Joseph Chamberlain and the "Unauthorized Programme"', *EHR*, 65 (Oct. 1950), 477–91.

653 —— 'Joseph Chamberlain, Parnell, and the Irish "Central Board" scheme, 1884–85', *IHS*, 8 (Sept. 1953), 324–61.

654 —— 'The Parnell manifesto of 21 November 1885 and the schools question', *EHR*, 62 (Jan. 1947), 42–51.

655 Hurst, Michael C. 'Joseph Chamberlain, the Conservatives and the succession to John Bright, 1886–89', *Hist.J.*, 7 (no. 1, 1964), 64–93.

656 Jones, Ieuan G. 'The election of 1868 in Merthyr Tydfil: a study in the politics of an industrial borough in the mid-nineteenth century', *JMH*, 33 (Sept. 1961), 270–86.

657 —— 'The Liberation Society and Welsh politics, 1844 to 1868', *Welsh History Review*, 1 (no. 2, 1961), 193–224.

658 Jones, J. R. 'The Conservatives and Gladstone in 1855', *EHR*, 77 (Jan. 1962), 95–8.

659 Jordan, H. Donaldson. 'Richard Cobden and penny postage: a note on the processes of reform', *VS*, 8 (June 1965), 355–60.

660 Kegal, C. H. 'Lord John Manners and the Young England movement: romanticism in politics', *Western Political Quarterly*, 14 (Sept. 1961), 691–8.

661 Kellas, James G. 'The Liberal party and the Scottish church disestablishment crisis', *EHR*, 79 (Jan. 1964), 31–46.

662 —— 'The Liberal party in Scotland 1876–1895', *SHR*, 44 (Apr. 1965), 1–16.

663 Kelley, Robert L. 'Midlothian: a study in politics and ideas', *VS*, 4 (Dec. 1960), 119–40.

664 Kemp, Betty. 'Reflections on the repeal of the Corn Laws', *VS*, 5 (Mar. 1962), 189–204.

665 Large, David. 'The House of Lords and Ireland in the age of Peel, 1832–1850', *IHS*, 9 (Sept. 1955), 367–99. Shows the extent of Irish landowning among peers.

666 Larkin, Emmet. 'Launching the counter-attack: part II of the Roman Catholic hierarchy and the destruction of Parnellism', *Review of Politics*, 28 (July 1966), 359–83.

667 —— 'Mounting the counter-attack: the Roman Catholic hierarchy and the destruction of Parnellism', *Review of Politics*, 25 (Apr. 1963), 157–82.

668 —— 'The Roman Catholic hierarchy and the fall of Parnell', *VS*, 4 (June 1961), 315–36.

669 Lawson-Tancred, Mary. 'The Anti-League and the Corn Law crisis of 1846', *Hist.J.*, 3 (no. 2, 1960), 162–83.

670 Leathes, Stanley. 'Great Britain', in *CMH*, XII, 23–64.

671 Lewis, Clyde J. 'Theory and expediency in Disraeli's policy', *VS*, 4 (Mar. 1961), 237–58.

672 Lloyd, Trevor. 'Uncontested seats in British general elections, 1852–1910', *Hist.J.*, 8 (no. 2, 1965), 260–5.

673 Lovett, Harrington V. 'The home government, 1858–1918', in *CHBE*, v, 206–25.

674 Lyons, Francis S. L. 'The economic ideas of Parnell', in *Historical studies: II, Papers, read to the third Conference of Irish Historians. 1959*, pp. 60–75.

675 McCaffrey, Lawrence J. 'Home rule and the general election of 1874 in Ireland', *IHS*, 9 (Sept. 1954), 190–212.

676 McCord, Norman. 'Cobden and Bright in politics, 1846–1857', in *Id. & Inst.*, pp. 87–114.

677 —— 'Some difficulties of parliamentary reform', *Hist.J.*, 10 (no. 3, 1967), 376–90.

678 McCord, Norman and A. E. Carrick. 'Northumberland and the general election of 1852', *Northern History*, 1 (1966), 92–108.

679 McCord, Norman and P. A. Wood. 'The Sunderland election of 1845', *Durham University Journal*, new ser., **21** (Dec. 1959), 11–21.

680 McGill, Barry. 'Francis Schnadhorst and Liberal party organization', *JMH*, **34** (Mar. 1962), 19–39.

681 Maehl, William H. 'Gladstone, the liberals and the election of 1874', *BIHR*, **36** (May 1963), 53–69.

682 —— 'The Liberal party and the Newcastle elections of 1874', *Durham University Journal*, new ser., **26** (June 1965), 148–58.

683 Mallalieu, William C. 'Joseph Chamberlain and workmen's compensation', *JEcH*, **10** (May 1950), 45–57.

684 Mather, Frederick C. 'Chartism: the present position of historical studies', in John S. Bromley and E. H. Kossmann (eds.). *Britain and the Netherlands*, II. Groningen, 1964, pp. 181–204.

685 Moody, Theodore W. 'The Irish university question in the nineteenth century', *History*, **43** (June 1958), 90–109.

686 —— 'Michael Davitt, 1846–1906: a survey and an appreciation', *Studies*, **35** (June, Sept., Dec. 1946), 199–208, 325–34, 433–8. Sympathetic.

687 —— 'Michael Davitt and the British labour movement, 1882–1906', *TRHS*, 5th ser., **4** (1953), 53–76.

688 —— 'The new departure in Irish politics, 1878–79', in Henry A. Cronne, Theodore W. Moody and D. B. Quinn (eds.). *Essays in British and Irish history in honour of James Eadie Todd*. 1949, pp. 303–33.

689 —— 'Parnell and the Galway election of 1886', *IHS*, **9** (Mar. 1955), 319–38.

690 Morgan, Kenneth O. 'Gladstone and Wales', *Welsh History Review*, **1** (1960), 65–82.

691 Mosse, George L. 'The Anti-League: 1844–1846', *EcHR*, **17** (no. 2, 1947), 134–42.

692 Mowat, Charles L. 'The approach to the welfare state in Great Britain', *AHR*, **58** (Oct. 1952), 55–63.

693 Mulvey, Helen F. 'Sir Charles Gavan Duffy: young Irelander and imperial statesman', *Canadian Historical Review*, **33** (Dec. 1952), 369–86.

694 Nowlan, Kevin B. 'The meaning of repeal in Irish history', in *Historical studies: IV, Papers read to the fifth Irish Conference of Historians*. 1963, pp. 1–17.

695 O'Higgins, Rachel. 'The Irish influence in the chartist movement', *PP*, **20** (Nov. 1961), 83–96.

696 —— 'Irish trade unions and politics, 1830–1850', *Hist.J.*, **4** (no. 1, 1961), 208–17.

697 O'Neill, James E. 'The Victorian background to the British welfare state', *South Atlantic Quarterly*, **66** (Spring 1967), 204–17.

698 Pelling, Henry. 'H. H. Champion: pioneer of labour representation', *Cambridge Journal*, **6** (Jan. 1953), 222–38.

699 Punnett, R. M. 'The parliamentary and personal backgrounds of British prime ministers, 1812 to 1963', *Quarterly Review*, **302** (July 1964), 254–66. Includes useful tables.

700 Reeder, David A. 'The politics of urban leaseholds in late Victorian England', *IRSH*, **6** (pt. 3, 1961), 413–30.

701 Roberts, David. 'Tory paternalism and social reform in early Victorian England', *AHR*, **63** (Jan. 1958), 323–37. Contends that the Tory reformers have been overrated.

702 Robinson, Ronald E. 'Imperial problems in British politics, 1880–1895', *CHBE*, III, 127–80.

703 Roche, Kennedy F. 'The relations of the Catholic Church and the state in England and Ireland, 1800–1852', *Historical Studies: III, Papers read before the fourth Irish Conference of Historians*. 1961, pp. 9–24.

704 Rose, Michael E. 'The anti-Poor Law movement in the north of England', *Northern History*, **1** (1966), 70–91.

705 Rowe, D. J. 'Chartism and the Spitalfields silk-weavers', *EcHR*, 2nd ser., **20** (Dec. 1967), 482–93.

706 —— 'The London Working Men's Association and the "People's Charter"', *PP*, **36** (Apr. 1967), 73–86.

707 Savage, D. C. 'Scottish politics, 1885–86', *SHR*, **40** (Oct. 1961), 118–35. The break-up of the Liberal party.

708 —— 'The origins of the Ulster Unionist party, 1885–6', *IHS*, **12** (Mar. 1961), 185–208.

709 Spinner, Thomas J., Jr. 'George Joachim Goschen: the man Lord Randolph Churchill "forgot"', *JMH*, **39** (Dec. 1967), 405–24.

710 Spring, David. 'Earl Fitzwilliam and the Corn Laws', *AHR*, **59** (Jan. 1954), 287–304.

711 Stuart, C. H. 'The formation of the coalition government of 1852', *TRHS*, 5th ser., **4** (1954), 45–68.

712 Tholfsen, Trygve R. 'The chartist crisis in Birmingham', *IRSH*, **3** (pt. 3, 1958), 461–80.

713 —— 'The origins of the Birmingham caucus', *Hist.J.*, **2** (no. 2, 1959), 161–84.

714 —— 'The transition to democracy in Victorian England', *IRSH*, **6** (pt. 2, 1961), 226–48. Shows working-class acceptance of middle-class leadership.

715 Thomas, J. Alun. 'The system of registration and the development of party organisation, 1832–70', *History*, **35** (Feb.–June 1950), 81–98.

716 Thompson, Francis M. L. 'Whigs and Liberals in West Riding, 1830–1860', *EHR*, **74** (Apr. 1959), 214–39.

717 Thompson, Paul. 'Liberals, radicals and labour in London 1880–1900', *PP*, **27** (Apr. 1964), 73–101.

718 Thornley, David. 'The Irish Conservatives and home rule, 1869–1873', *IHS*, **11** (Mar. 1959), 200–22.

719 —— 'The Irish home rule party and parliamentary obstruction, 1874–1887', *IHS*, **12** (Mar. 1960), 38–57.

720 Tierney, Michael. 'Origin and growth of modern Irish nationalism', *Studies*, **30** (Sept. 1941), 321–36. From a nationalist standpoint.

721 Urwin, Derek W. 'The development of the Conservative party organisation in Scotland until 1912', *SHR*, **44** (Oct. 1965), 89–111.

722 Vincent, John R. 'The electoral sociology of Rochdale', *EcHR*, 2nd ser., **16** (Aug. 1963), 76–90.

723 Walpole, Spencer. 'Great Britain, last years of Whiggism, parliamentary reform (1856–68)', in *CMH*, XI, 325–46.

724 Ward, John T. 'The factory reform movement in Scotland', *SHR*, **41** (Oct. 1962), 100–23.

725 —— 'West Riding landowners and the Corn Laws', *EHR*, **81** (Apr. 1966), 256–72.

726 Whyte, John H. 'Daniel O'Connell and the repeal party', *IHS*, **11** (Sept. 1959), 297–316.

727 —— 'The influence of the Catholic clergy on elections in nineteenth century Ireland', *EHR*, **75** (Apr. 1960), 239–59.

728 —— 'Landlord influence at elections in Ireland, 1760–1885', *EHR*, **80** (Oct. 1965), 740–60.

729 Wilkins, M. S. 'The non-socialist origins of England's first important socialist organization', *IRSH*, **4** (pt. 2, 1959), 199–207.

730 Williams, Philip M. 'Public opinion and the railway rates question in 1886', *EHR*, **67** (Jan. 1952), 37–73. A reply to (573).

731 Winter, James. 'The cave of Adullam and parliamentary reform', *EHR*, **81** (Jan. 1966), 38–55.

732 Zebel, Sidney H. 'Fair trade: an English reaction to the breakdown of the Cobden treaty system', *JMH*, **12** (June 1940), 161–85.

VI FOREIGN RELATIONS

1 Printed sources

733 Blakiston, Noel (ed.). *The Roman question. Extracts from the despatches of Odo Russell from Rome 1858–1870.* 1962.

734 *British and foreign state papers, with which is incorporated Hertslet's 'Commercial treaties', 1812/14–.* 1815–. Annual.

735 Curato, Federico (ed.). *Le relazioni diplomatiche fra la Gran Bretagna e il regno di Sardegna dal 1852 al 1856; il carteggio diplomatico di Sir James Hudson.* Turin, 1956.

736 *Diplomatic and consular reports: annual series.* 1886–1916.

737 *Diplomatic and consular reports: miscellaneous series.* 1886–1910, 22 vols.

738 Gooch, George P. and Harold Temperley (eds.). *British documents on the origins of the war, 1898–1914,* I, *The end of British isolation.* 1926. Covers Dec. 1897–Apr. 1904.

739 Hertslet, Sir Edward (ed.). *The map of Europe by treaty: showing the various political and territorial changes which have taken place since the general peace of 1814.* 1875–91, 4 vols.

740 Joll, James B. (ed.). *Britain and Europe: Pitt to Churchill, 1793–1940.* 1950.

741 Knaplund, Paul (ed.). *Letters from the Berlin embassy, 1871–4, 1880–5* (Annual report of the American Historical Association, II). Washington, 1942.

742 Loftus, Lord Augustus W. F. S. *The diplomatic reminiscences of Lord Augustus Loftus, P.C., G.C.B.* 1892–4, 4 vols. Covers 1837–79, not too profoundly.

743 Temperley, Harold W. V. and Lillian M. Penson (eds.). *Foundations of British foreign policy from Pitt (1792) to Salisbury (1902); or documents, old and new, selected and edited, with historical introductions.* Cambridge, 1938.

2 Surveys

744 Gooch, George P. and Adolphus W. Ward (eds.). *Cambridge history of British foreign policy, 1783–1919.* Cambridge, 1922–3, 3 vols.

745 Seton-Watson, Robert W. *Britain in Europe, 1789–1914, a survey of foreign policy,* 2nd ed. Cambridge, 1955. The standard general study.

746 Strang, William, 1st Baron. *Britain in world affairs: a survey of the fluctuations in British power and influence, Henry VIII to Elizabeth II.* 1961. An interesting interpretation of Britain's relative standing.

3 Monographs

747 Adams, Ephraim D. *Great Britain and the American civil war.* 1925, 2 vols.

748 Allen, Harry C. *The Anglo-American relationship since 1783.* 1959. Rev. ed. of *Great Britain and the United States: a history of Anglo-American relations, 1783–1952.* 1954.

749 Anderson, Matthew S. *The eastern question 1774–1923: a study in international relations.* 1966.

750 Bayer, Theodor. *England und der neue Kurs, 1890–1895.* Tübingen, 1955.

751 Beales, Derek. *England and Italy, 1859–60.* 1961. An excellent study in diplomacy and politics.

752 Bloch, Charles. *Les relations entre la France et la Grande Bretagne, 1871–1878.* Paris, 1955.

753 Bourne, Kenneth. *Britain and the balance of power in North America, 1815–1908.* Berkeley, 1967.

754 Brebner, John Bartlet. *The north Atlantic triangle: the interplay of Canada, the United States, and Great Britain.* New Haven, 1945.

755 Campbell, Alexander E. *Great Britain and the United States, 1895–1903.* 1960.

756 Campbell, Charles S., Jr. *Anglo-American understanding, 1898–1903.* Baltimore, 1957.

757 Costin, William C. *Great Britain and China, 1833–1860.* Oxford, 1937.
758 Ferns, Henry S. *Britain and Argentina in the nineteenth century.* Oxford, 1960.
759 Gleason, John H. *The genesis of Russophobia in Great Britain: a study of the interaction of policy and opinion.* Cambridge, Mass., 1950.
760 Gosses, Frans. *The management of British foreign policy before the first world war, especially during the period 1880–1914.* Leiden, 1948.
761 Grenville, John A. S. *Lord Salisbury and foreign policy: the close of the nineteenth century.* 1964.
762 Hall, John R. *England and the Orleans monarchy.* 1912.
763 Harris, David. *Britain and the Bulgarian horrors of 1876.* Chicago, 1939.
764 Headlam-Morley, James W. *Studies in diplomatic history,* ed. Agnes Headlam-Morley. 1930. Essays on selected problems, 1814–1919.
765 Henderson, Gavin B. *Crimean war diplomacy and other historical essays,* ed. William O. Henderson. Glasgow, 1947.
766 Hjelholt, Holger. *British mediation in the Danish-German conflict, 1848–1850,* vol. I. Copenhagen, 1965.
767 Howard, Christopher. *Splendid isolation: a study of ideas concerning Britain's international position and foreign policy during the later years of the third Marquess of Salisbury.* 1967.
768 Imlah, Ann G. *Britain and Switzerland, 1845–60: a study of Anglo-Swiss relations during some critical years for Swiss neutrality.* Hamden, Conn., 1966.
769 Jones, Wilbur D. *Lord Aberdeen and the Americas.* Athens, Ga., 1958.
770 Knaplund, Paul. *Gladstone's foreign policy.* 1935. Still the best study.
771 Langer, William L. *The diplomacy of imperialism 1890–1902,* 2nd ed. New York, 1960.
772 Lee, Dwight E. *Great Britain and the Cyprus convention policy of 1878.* Cambridge, Mass., 1934.
773 Lowe, Cedric J. *Salisbury and the Mediterranean, 1886–1896.* 1965.
774 Marriott, John A. R. *The eastern question,* 2nd ed. Oxford, 1918. Somewhat out of date; see (749).
775 Marsden, Arthur. *Britain and the end of the Tunis treaties (EHR,* supplement no. 1). 1965.
776 Medlicott, William N. *Bismarck, Gladstone, and the concert of Europe.* 1956.
777 —— *The congress of Berlin and after; a diplomatic history of the Near Eastern settlement, 1878–1880.* 1938.
778 Medlicott, William N. (ed.). *From Metternich to Hitler: aspects of British and foreign history, 1814–1939.* 1963. A collection of essays.
779 Millman, Richard. *British foreign policy and the coming of the Franco-Prussian war.* Oxford, 1965.
780 Mosse, Werner E. *The European powers and the German question, 1848–1871: with special reference to England and Russia.* 1958.
781 —— *The rise and fall of the Crimean system, 1855–1871: the story of a peace settlement.* 1963.
782 Neale, Robert G. *Great Britain and United States expansion: 1898–1900.* East Lansing, 1966.
783 Palm, Franklin C. *England and Napoleon III.* Durham, N.C., 1948.
784 Parry, Ernest J. *The Spanish marriages, 1841–1846; a study of the influence of dynastic ambition upon foreign policy.* 1936.
785 Poolman, Kenneth. *The Alabama incident.* 1958.
786 Přibram, Alfred F. *England and the international policy of the European great powers, 1871–1914.* Oxford, 1931.
787 Puryear, Vernon J. *England, Russia and the Straits question, 1844–1856.* Berkeley, 1931.
788 —— *International economics and diplomacy in the Near East: a study of British commercial policy in the Levant, 1834–1853.* Stanford, 1935.
789 Ramsay, Anna A. W. *Idealism and foreign policy; a study of the relations of Great Britain with Germany and France, 1860–1878.* 1925.
790 Rose, Saul. *Britain and south-east Asia.* 1962.
791 Sanderson, George N. *England, Europe and the upper Nile, 1882–1899; a study in the partition of Africa.* Edinburgh, 1965.

792 Seton-Watson, Robert W. *Disraeli, Gladstone and the eastern question: a study in diplomacy and party politics.* 1935.

793 Smith, Colin L. *The embassy of Sir William White at Constantinople, 1886–1891.* 1957.

794 Sontag, Raymond. *Germany and England: background of conflict, 1848–1894.* New York, 1938. A masterpiece not merely of diplomatic but also of cultural history.

795 Spender, John A. *Fifty years of Europe; a study in pre-war documents.* 1933. Begins with 1870.

796 Sproxton, Charles. *Palmerston and the Hungarian revolution; a dissertation.* Cambridge, 1919.

797 Steefel, Lawrence D. *The Schleswig-Holstein question.* Cambridge, Mass., 1932.

798 Taylor, Alan J. P. *The trouble makers: dissent over foreign policy, 1792–1939.* 1957. One of the better works of a brilliant writer.

799 Temperley, Harold W. V. *England and the Near East,* I, *The Crimea.* 1936.

800 Thistlethwaite, Frank. *The Anglo-American connection in the early nineteenth century.* Philadelphia, 1959.

801 Tischendorf, Alfred. *Great Britain and Mexico in the era of Porfirio Diaz.* Durham, N.C., 1961.

802 Urban, Miriam B. *British public opinion and policy on the unification of Italy, 1856–1861.* Scottdale, Pa., 1938.

803 Webster, Charles K. *The foreign policy of Palmerston, 1830–1841,* II. 1951.

804 Wehrle, Edmund S. *Britain, China, and the anti-missionary riots, 1891–1900.* Minneapolis, 1966.

805 Williams, Mary W. *Anglo-American Isthmian diplomacy, 1815–1915.* Washington, 1916.

4 Biographies

(See also sec. v, pt. 4, above.)

806 Byrne, Leo G. *The great ambassador: a study of the diplomatic career of the Right Honourable Stratford Canning, K.G., K.G.C.B., Viscount Stratford de Redcliffe, and the epoch during which he served as the British ambassador to the Sublime Porte of the Ottoman Sultan.* Columbus, 1964. Somewhat popular.

807 Cecil, Algernon. *British foreign secretaries, 1807–1916.* 1927.

808 Edwards, Henry S. *Sir William White, K.C.B., K.C.M.G., for six years ambassador at Constantinople: his life and correspondence.* 1902.

809 Fitzmaurice, Lord Edmond. *The life of Granville George Leveson Gower, second Earl Granville.* 1905, 2 vols. Useful also for political history.

810 Lane-Poole, Stanley. *The life of the Right Honourable Stratford Canning, Viscount Stratford de Redcliffe ... from his memoirs and private and official papers.* 1888, 2 vols.

811 Mowat, Robert B. *The life of Lord Pauncefote, first ambassador to the United States.* 1929.

812 Newton, Thomas W. L., 2nd Baron. *Lord Lyons: a record of British diplomacy.* 1913, 2 vols.

813 Smith, Elizabeth F. M. *The life of Stratford Canning, Lord Stratford de Redcliffe.* 1933.

814 Taffs, Winifred. *Ambassador to Bismarck, Lord Odo Russell.* 1938.

815 Wemyss, Victoria. *Memoirs and letters of the Right Hon. Sir Robert Morier, G.C.B., from 1826 to 1876.* 1911, 2 vols.

816 Zetland, Lawrence J. L. Dundas, 2nd Marquis of. *Lord Cromer; being the authorized life of Evelyn Baring, first Earl of Cromer.* 1932.

5 Articles

817 Adshead, S. A. M. 'Odo Russell and the first Vatican council', *Journal of Religious History,* 2 (Dec. 1963), 295–302.

818 Bartle, G. F. 'Bowring and the Near Eastern crisis of 1838–1840', *EHR,* 79 (Oct. 1964), 761–74.

819 Bourne, Kenneth. 'The Clayton–Bulwer treaty and the decline of British opposition to the territorial expansion of the United States, 1857–60', *JMH*, **33** (Sept. 1961), 287–91.

820 Case, Lynn M. 'A duel of giants in old Stambul: Stratford versus Thouvenel', *JMH*, **35** (Sept. 1963), 262–73. Includes documents.

821 Cook, Adrian. 'A lost opportunity in Anglo-American relations: the Alabama claims, 1865–1867', *Australian Journal of Politics and History*, **12** (April 1966), 54–65.

822 Cowling, Maurice. 'Lytton, the cabinet, and the Russians, August to November 1878', *EHR*, **76** (Jan. 1961), 59–79.

823 Cromwell, Valerie. 'The private member of the House of Commons and foreign policy in the nineteenth century', in *Liber memorialis Sir Maurice Powicke: studies presented to the International Commission for the History of Representative Institutions*, XXVII. Louvain, 1965, pp. 193–218.

824 Davies, Godfrey. 'The pattern of British foreign policy, 1815–1914', *Huntington Library Quarterly*, **6** (May 1943), 367–77.

825 Dwyer, Frederick J. 'R. A. Cross and the eastern crisis of 1875–8', *Slavonic and East European Review*, **39** (June 1961), 440–58.

826 Florescu, Radu R. 'Stratford Canning, Palmerston, and the Wallachian revolution of 1848', *JMH*, **35** (Sept. 1963), 227–44.

827 Gillard, D. R. 'Salisbury's African policy and the Heligoland offer of 1890', *EHR*, **75** (Oct. 1960), 631–53.

828 Grenville, John A. S. 'Goluchowski, Salisbury, and the Mediterranean agreements, 1895–1897', *Slavonic and East European Review*, **36** (June 1958), 340–69.

829 Hinsley, Francis H. 'British foreign policy and colonial questions, 1895–1904', in *CHBE*, III, 490–537.

830 —— 'International rivalry, 1885–1895', in *CHBE*, III, 255–92.

831 —— 'International rivalry in the colonial sphere, 1869–1885', in *CHBE*, III, 95–126.

832 Howard, Christopher. 'The policy of isolation', *Hist.J.*, **10** (no. 1, 1967), 77–88.

833 —— 'Splendid isolation', *History*, **47** (Feb. 1962), 32–41.

834 Jefferson, Margaret M. 'Lord Salisbury and the eastern question', *Slavonic and East European Review*, **39** (Dec. 1960), 44–60.

835 Jones, Robert H. 'Anglo-American relations, 1861–1865, reconsidered', *Mid-America*, **45** (Jan. 1963), 36–49.

836 Khasigian, Amos. 'Economic factors and British neutrality, 1861–1865', *Historian*, **25** (Aug. 1963), 451–65.

837 Lowe, Cedric J. 'Anglo-Italian differences over East Africa, 1892–1895, and their effects upon the Mediterranean entente', *EHR*, **81** (Apr. 1966), 315–36.

838 Miller, T. B. 'The Egyptian question and British foreign policy, 1892–1894', *JMH*, **32** (Mar. 1960), 1–15.

839 Mosse, Werner E. 'The end of the Crimean system: England, Russia and the neutrality of the Black Sea, 1870–1', *Hist.J.*, **4** (no. 2, 1961), 164–90.

840 —— 'Public opinion and foreign policy: the British public and the war-scare of November 1870', *Hist.J.*, **6** (no. 1, 1963), 38–58.

841 —— 'Queen Victoria and her ministers in the Schleswig-Holstein crisis 1863–1864', *EHR*, **78** (Apr. 1963), 263–83.

842 Murray, John. 'Britain and Argentina in the nineteenth century', *Studies*, **49** (Winter 1960), 420–36.

843 Penson, Lillian M. 'The new course in British foreign policy, 1892–1902', *TRHS*, 4th ser., **25** (1943), 121–38.

844 Ramm, Agatha. 'The Crimean war', in *NCMH*, X, 468–92.

845 Robson, Maureen M. 'The *Alabama* claims and the Anglo-American reconciliation, 1865–71', *Canadian Historical Review*, **42** (Mar. 1961), 1–22.

846 —— 'Lord Clarendon and the Cretan question, 1868–9', *Hist.J.*, **3** (no. 1, 1960), 38–55.

847 Rodríguez, Mario. 'The "Prometheus" and the Clayton–Bulwer treaty', *JMH*, **36** (Sept. 1964), 260–78.

848 Sanderson, George N. 'The Anglo-German agreement of 1890 and the Upper Nile', *EHR*, **78** (Jan. 1963), 49–72.
849 —— 'England, Italy, the Nile valley and the European balance, 1890–91', *Hist.J.*, **7** (no. 1, 1964), 94–119.
850 Simpson, F. A. 'England and the Italian war of 1859', *Hist.J.*, **5** (no. 2, 1962), 111–21.
851 Walker, Franklin A. 'The rejection of Stratford Canning by Nicholas I', *BIHR*, **40** (May 1967), 50–64.
852 Walpole, Spencer. 'Great Britain and the Crimean war (1852–6)', in *CMH*, XI, 309–24.
853 Weber, Frank G. 'Palmerston and Prussian liberalism, 1848', *JMH*, **35** (June 1963), 125–36.

VII SOCIAL HISTORY

1 Printed sources
(See also sec. VIII, pt. 1, below.)

854 Adburgham, Alison (ed.). *A Punch history of manners and modes, 1841–1940.* 1961. Pictures and commentary from *Punch*, by years.
855 *Annual reports of the Registrar-General for England and Wales.* 1837/8–1920. The basic source for demography. See also the decennial supplementary volumes, *Mortality in England and Wales.* 1862–1912.
856 Bateman, John. *The great landowners of Great Britain and Ireland.* 4th ed., 1883. The 'new Domesday Book' for large landholdings.
857 Bessborough, Vere B. Ponsonby, 9th Earl of (ed.). *Lady Charlotte Guest 1833–1852.* 1950. Extracts from her journal.
858 —— *Lady Charlotte Schreiber, 1853–1891.* 1952.
859 Booth, Charles. *Life and labour of the people of London.* 1902–3, 17 vols. First-rate amateur sociology, a comprehensive study of poverty, begun in 1889.
860 Booth, William. *In darkest England and the way out.* 1890. A study of poverty by the founder of the Salvation Army.
861 Chadwick, Edwin. *Report on the sanitary condition of the labouring population of Great Britain*, ed. Michael W. Flinn. Edinburgh, 1965. A classic report, written in 1842.
862 Engels, Friedrich. *The condition of the working classes in England*, tr. William O. Henderson and William H. Chaloner. Oxford, 1958. Written in 1842.
863 Evans, Joan (ed.). *The Victorians.* 1966. Contemporary comments on the social scene, with some introductory narrative.
864 Fulford, Roger (ed.). *Dearest child: letters between Queen Victoria and the Princess Royal, 1858–1861.* 1964.
865 Graves, Charles L. (ed.). *Mr. Punch's history of modern England.* 1921–2, 4 vols. Cartoons and commentary.
866 Kelly, Edith and Thomas (eds.). *A schoolmaster's notebook, being an account of a nineteenth-century experiment in social welfare.* Manchester, 1958. The notebook of David Winstanley.
867 Kyd, James G. (ed.). *Scottish population statistics.* Edinburgh, 1952.
868 Lutyens, Mary (ed.). *Lady Lytton's court diary, 1895–1899.* 1961.
869 Mackerness, Eric D. (ed.). *The journals of George Sturt, 1890–1927: a selection*, I, *1890–1904.* Cambridge, 1967. Interesting for village life. See (1181).
870 Maclure, J. Stuart (ed.). *Educational documents: England and Wales, 1816–1963.* 1965.
871 Marchant, James (ed.). *The declining birth rate; its causes and effects, being the report of and the chief evidence taken by the National Birth-Rate Commission . . . 1916.*
872 Mayhew, Henry. *London labour and the London poor: a cyclopedia of the conditions and earnings of those that will work, those that cannot work, and those that will not work.* 4 vols., 1861–2. A masterpiece of reporting, originally published as articles in the *Morning Chronicle*, 1849–50.

873 Pike, Edgar R. (ed.). *Human documents of the industrial revolution in Britain.* 1966. Eyewitness accounts, mainly from Blue Books.
874 —— *Human documents of the Victorian golden age (1850–1875).* 1967.
875 Raverat, Gwen. *Period piece; a Cambridge childhood.* 1952. Charming auto-biography of Darwin's granddaughter, born 1885.

2 Surveys

876 Checkland, Sydney G. *The rise of industrial society in England, 1815–1885.* 1964. An excellent social and economic history, with an extensive biblio-graphy.
877 Fay, Charles R. *Life and labour in the nineteenth century.* Cambridge, 1920.
878 Gregg, Pauline. *A social and economic history of Britain, 1760–1960.* 1962.
879 Quennell, Marjorie and Charles H. B. *A history of everyday things in England,* rev. ed. by Peter Quennell, vols. III–IV. 1957–60.
880 Reader, William J. *Life in Victorian England.* 1964.
881 Traill, Henry D. (ed.). *Social England, a record of the progress of the people in religion, laws, learning, arts, industry, commerce, science, literature, and manners . . . VI, From the battle of Waterloo to the general election of 1885.* 1897.
882 Trevelyan, George M. *English social history.* 3rd ed., 1946. A classic, delightful but outdated for this period.

3 Monographs

(See also sec. VIII, pt. 3, and sec. XII, pt. 3, below.)

883 Abel-Smith, Brian. *A history of the nursing profession.* 1960.
884 —— *The hospitals, 1800–1948: a study in social administration in England and Wales.* 1964.
885 Adams, William F. *Ireland and the Irish emigration to the new world from 1815 to the famine.* 1932.
886 Adamson, John W. *English education, 1789–1902.* Cambridge, 1930. A respectable survey.
887 Adburgham, Alison. *Shops and shopping, 1800–1914.* 1964.
888 Altick, Richard D. *The English common reader: a social history of the mass reading public, 1800–1900.* 1957. An important study.
889 Anderson, C. Arnold and Miriam Schnaper. *School and society in England: social backgrounds of Oxford and Cambridge students.* Washington, 1952.
890 Archer, Richard L. *Secondary education in the nineteenth century.* Cambridge, 1921.
891 Argles, Michael. *South Kensington to Robbins: an account of English technical and scientific education since 1851.* 1964.
892 Armytage, Walter H. G. *Four hundred years of English education.* Cambridge, 1964.
893 —— *Heavens below: Utopian experiments in England, 1560–1960.* 1961.
894 —— *The rise of the technocrats: a social history.* 1965.
895 —— *A social history of engineering.* 1961.
896 Ashworth, William. *The genesis of modern British town planning: a study in the economic and social history of the nineteenth and twentieth centuries.* 1954.
897 Aslin, Elizabeth. *Nineteenth-century English furniture.* 1962.
898 Balfour, Graham. *The educational systems of Great Britain and Ireland.* 2nd ed., Oxford, 1903.
899 Bamford, Thomas W. *Rise of the public schools: a study of boys' public boarding schools in England and Wales from 1837 to the present.* 1967.
900 Banks, Joseph A. *Prosperity and parenthood: a study of family planning among the Victorian middle classes.* 1954. An interesting study of birth control and the decline of family size in the late nineteenth century.
901 Banks, Joseph A. and Olive. *Feminism and family planning in Victorian England.* Liverpool, 1964.

902 Barker, Theodore C. and John R. Harris. *A Merseyside town in the industrial revolution: St. Helens 1750–1900.* Liverpool, 1954. A good local history.
903 Barnard, Howard C. *A short history of English education from 1760 to 1944.* 1947.
904 Bell, Aldon D. *London in the age of Dickens* (The Centers of Civilization Series, XXIII). Norman, Okla., 1967.
905 Bellman, Harold. *Bricks and mortals; a study of the building society movement and the story of the Abbey National Society, 1849–1949.* 1949.
906 Benevolo, Leonardo. *The origins of modern town planning,* tr. Judith Landry. 1967.
907 Birchenough, Charles. *History of elementary education in England and Wales from 1800 to the present day.* Rev. ed., 1938.
908 Boner, Harold A. *Hungry generations: the nineteenth century case against Malthusianism.* New York, 1955. Stresses the problem of overpopulation.
909 Bosanquet, Helen. *Social work in London, 1869 to 1912: a history of the Charity Organisation Society.* 1914. See also (1021).
910 Bovill, Edward W. *The England of Nimrod and Surtees, 1815–1854.* 1959. On the great days of coaching.
911 Briggs, Asa. *Victorian cities.* 1964.
912 Briggs, Asa and Conrad Gill. *History of Birmingham.* Oxford, 1952, 2 vols. A major example of urban history; Gill covers the period before 1865, Briggs after 1865.
913 Brittain, Vera M. *The women at Oxford: a fragment of history.* 1960.
914 Brooke, Iris and James Laver. *English costume in the nineteenth century.* 1947.
915 Buck, Anne M. *Victorian costume and costume accessories.* 1961.
916 Burgess, Henry J. *Enterprise in education: the story of the work of the established Church in the education of the people prior to 1870.* 1958.
917 Burke, John B. *A genealogical and heraldic history of the peerage, baronetage and knightage,* ed. Peter Townsend. 103rd ed., 1963. Also known as *Burke's peerage.*
918 —— *Genealogical and heraldic history of the landed gentry,* ed. Peter Townsend. 18th ed., 1965. Also known as *Burke's landed gentry.*
919 Burnett, John. *Plenty and want: a social history of diet in England from 1815 to the present day.* 1966.
920 Campbell, Roy H. *Scotland since 1707: the rise of an industrial society.* Oxford, 1965.
921 Carrier, Norman H. and James R. Jeffery. *External migration: a study of the available statistics, 1815–1950.* 1953.
922 Carrothers, William A. *Emigration from the British isles, with special reference to the development of the overseas dominions.* 1929.
923 Carr-Saunders, Alexander M. and Paul A. Wilson. *The professions.* Oxford, 1933. Studies the development of the various professions.
924 Carter, Henry. *The English temperance movement: a study in objectives.* 1933.
925 Chadwick, George F. *The park and the town; public landscape in the 19th and 20th centuries.* 1966. On the history of landscape architecture and parks.
926 Chadwick, Owen. *Victorian miniature.* 1960. An interesting sketch of the relation of parson and squire in Ketteringham.
927 Chaloner, William H. *The social and economic development of Crewe, 1780–1923.* Manchester, 1950. A meticulous study of the growth of a railroad centre.
928 Chastenet, Jacques. *La vie quotidienne en Angleterre au début du regne de Victoria (1837–1851).* Paris, 1961.
929 Clark, Ronald W. *The Victorian mountaineers.* 1953.
930 Clark-Kennedy, Archibald E. *The London: a study in the voluntary hospital system.* 1962–3, 2 vols.
931 C[okayne], G[eorge] E. *The complete peerage of England, Scotland, Ireland, Great Britain and the United Kingdom, extant, extinct, or dormant,* rev. by Vicary Gibbs. New ed., 1910–59, 13 vols. in 14. Originally published 1887–98, the best guide to the peerage, with interesting appendices.
932 Cole, George D. H. *Studies in class structure.* 1955.

933 Cole, George D. H. and Raymond W. Postgate. *The common people 1746–1946*. 2nd ed., 1946. A monument of social history.

934 Coleman, Terry. *The railway navvies*. 1965.

935 Connell, Kenneth H. *The population of Ireland 1750–1845*. Oxford, 1950.

936 Cope, Zachary. *Six disciples of Florence Nightingale*. 1961.

937 Cotgrove, Stephen F. *Technical education and social change*. 1958.

938 Cousens, S. H. *The regional variation in mortality during the great Irish famine* (Proceedings of the Royal Irish Academy, LXIII). Dublin, 1963.

939 Cruickshank, Marjorie. *Church and state in English education: 1870 to the present day*. 1963.

940 Cunnington, C. Willett. *English women's clothing in the nineteenth century*. 1937.

941 —— *Feminine attitudes in the nineteenth century*. 1936.

942 Cunnington, C. Willett and Phyllis. *Handbook of English costume in the nineteenth century*. 1959. Illustrated.

943 Cunnington, Phyllis and Anne Buck. *Children's costume in England, from the fourteenth to the end of the nineteenth century*. 1965.

944 Curtis, Stanley J. *History of education in Great Britain*. 3rd ed., 1953. A standard survey.

945 Curtis, Stanley J. and Myrtle E. A. Boultwood. *An introductory history of English education since 1800*. 1960.

946 Dainton, Courtney. *The story of England's hospitals*. 1961.

947 Darton, Frederick J. H. *Children's books in England: five centuries of social life*. 2nd ed., Cambridge, 1959.

948 Davies, Cecil S. (ed.). *A history of Macclesfield*. Manchester, 1961.

949 Dewsnup, Ernest R. *The housing problem in England: its statistics, legislation and policy*. Manchester, 1907.

950 Dodds, John W. *The age of paradox: a biography of England 1841–1851*. New York, 1952. An interesting potpourri of Victoriana.

951 Doubleday, Herbert A. (ed.). *The Victoria history of the counties of England*. 1900–. Valuable for local history.

952 Dunbar, Janet. *The early Victorian woman: some aspects of her life, 1837–57*. 1953.

953 Dury, George H. *The east midlands and the Peak*, II, *1800–1900*. 1963.

954 Dutton, Ralph. *The Victorian home: some aspects of nineteenth-century taste and manners*. 1954.

955 Dyos, Harold J. *Victorian suburb: a study of the growth of Camberwell*. Leicester, 1961. A masterful local history.

956 Ede, John F. *History of Wednesbury*. Wednesbury, 1962.

957 Edwards, R. Dudley and T. Desmond Williams (eds.). *The great famine: studies in Irish history, 1845–1852*. Dublin, 1956. The most important scholarly study.

958 Fay, Charles R. *The Corn Laws and social England*. Cambridge, 1932.

959 Ferguson, Thomas. *The dawn of Scottish social welfare: a survey from medieval times to 1863*. 1948.

960 —— *Scottish social welfare, 1864–1914*. Edinburgh, 1958. Emphasizes the medical aspect.

961 Ffrench, Yvonne. *The great exhibition, 1851*. 1950. See also (971).

962 Freeman, Thomas W. *The conurbations of Great Britain*. Manchester, 1959.

963 Fryer, Peter. *Mrs. Grundy: studies in English prudery*. 1963.

964 Fussell, George E. *The English rural labourer: his home, furniture, clothing and food from Tudor to Victorian times*. 1949.

965 Fussell, George E. and Kathleen R. *The English countryman: his life and work, A.D. 1500–1900*. 1955.

966 —— *The English countrywoman: a farmhouse social history, A.D. 1500–1900*. 1953.

967 Gartner, Lloyd P. *The Jewish immigrant in England 1870–1914*. 1960.

968 Gaskell, Philip. *Morvern transformed: a highland parish in the nineteenth century*. Cambridge, 1968.

969 Gernsheim, Alison. *Fashion and reality, 1890–1914*. 1963.

970 Gibbs-Smith, Charles H. *The fashionable lady in the 19th century*. 1960.

971 —— *The great exhibition of 1851*. 1950. Probably the best study.

972 Glass, David V. *Population policies and movements in Europe.* 1940. Useful on birth control.
973 Glass, David V. and David E. C. Eversley (eds.). *Population in history: essays in historical demography.* 1965.
974 Glass, Ruth D. (ed.). *London: aspects of change.* 1964.
975 Grinsell, Leslie V., H. B. Wells, H. S. Tallamy and John Betjeman. *Studies in the history of Swindon.* Swindon, 1950.
976 Hammond, John L. and Barbara. *The age of the chartists, 1832–1854: a study in discontent.* 1930. A Fabian classic, heavily biased. A shorter version is *The bleak age.* 1934.
977 Handley, James E. *The Irish in modern Scotland.* Cork, 1947. Valuable also for the history of industrialization.
978 Harrison, John F. C. *A history of the Working Men's College, 1854–1954.* 1954.
979 —— *Learning and living, 1790–1960: a study in the history of the English adult education movement.* 1961. A useful contribution.
980 Harrison, Michael. *London by gaslight, 1861–1911.* 1963.
981 Hasbach, Wilhelm. *A history of the English agricultural labourer*, tr. Ruth Kenyon. 1908. A careful monograph, first published 1894.
982 Hewitt, Margaret. *Wives and mothers in Victorian industry.* 1958. A useful and judicious study.
983 Hobhouse, Christopher. *1851 and the Crystal Palace.* Rev. ed., 1950.
984 Hobsbawm, Eric J. *Labouring men: studies in the history of labour.* 1964. An important contribution.
985 —— *Primitive rebels. Studies in archaic forms of social movement in the 19th and 20th centuries.* Manchester, 1959. Includes a chapter on labour sects.
986 Hole, Christina. *English sports and pastimes.* 1949.
987 Hollis, Christopher. *Eton, a history.* 1960.
988 Hoskins, William G. *The midland peasant: the economic and social history of a Leicestershire village.* 1959. The village is Wigston Magna.
989 Ilchester, Giles S. H. Fox-Strangways, 6th Earl of. *Chronicles of Holland House, 1820–1900.* 1937. On the Fox family, Lords Holland.
990 Innes, John W. *Class fertility trends in England and Wales, 1876–1934.* Cambridge, 1938.
991 Jackson, John A. *The Irish in Britain.* 1963. A pioneering but not definitive study in historical sociology.
992 Johnson, Leonard G. *The social evolution of industrial Britain; a study in the growth of our industrial society.* Liverpool, 1959.
993 Jones, Kathleen. *Mental health and social policy, 1845–1959.* 1960.
994 Kamm, Josephine. *Hope deferred.* 1965. A history of female education.
995 —— *Rapiers and battleaxes: the women's movement and its aftermath.* 1966.
996 Kelly, Thomas. *Early public libraries: a history of public libraries in Great Britain before 1850.* 1966.
997 —— *A history of adult education in Great Britain.* Liverpool, 1962.
998 Laver, James. *The age of optimism: manners and morals 1848–1914.* 1966.
999 —— *Taste and fashion: from the French Revolution to the present day.* New ed., 1946.
1000 —— *Victorian vista.* 1954. On manners and fashions.
1001 Lewis, Roy and Angus Maude. *The English middle classes.* 1949. A learned and interesting little volume.
1002 Lipman, Vivian D. *Social history of the Jews in England 1850–1950.* 1954.
1003 Lochhead, Marion. *Their first ten years: Victorian childhood.* 1956.
1004 —— *The Victorian household.* 1964.
1005 —— *Young Victorians.* 1959. A sequel to (1003), dealing with adolescence.
1006 Lockwood, David. *The blackcoated worker: a study in class consciousness.* 1958. An interesting study of the clerks.
1007 Longmate, Norman. *King cholera: the biography of a disease.* 1966.
1008 Lowndes, George A. N. *The silent social revolution; an account of the expansion of public education in England and Wales, 1895–1935.* 1937.
1009 McGregor, Oliver R. *Divorce in England, a centenary study.* 1957. Excellent social history.

1010 Mack, Edward C. *Public schools, 1780 to 1860: an examination of the relationship between contemporary ideas and the evolution of an English institution.* 1938.

1011 —— *Public schools and British opinion since 1860: the relationship between contemporary ideas and the evolution of an English institution.* New York, 1941.

1012 Marcus, Steven. *The other Victorians: a study of sexuality and pornography in mid-nineteenth-century England.* New York, 1966. A pioneering study of pornography, employing literary analysis and Freudian psychology. See the review article by Brian Harrison, *VS*, **10** (Mar. 1967), 239–62.

1013 Marsh, David C. *The changing social structure of England and Wales, 1871–1951.* 1958.

1014 Martin, Ernest W. *Where London ends: English provincial life after 1750, being an account of the English country town and the lives, works, and development of provincial people through a period of two hundred years.* 1958.

1015 Martin, Robert B. *Enter rumour: four early Victorian scandals.* 1962. The cases of Lady Flora Hastings, the Master of St Cross Hospital, the Eglinton tournament and George Hudson.

1016 Mitchell, Rosamund J. and Mary D. R. Leys. *A history of London life.* 1958.

1017 Moers, Ellen. *The dandy: Brummell to Beerbohm.* 1960.

1018 Moody, Theodore W. and James C. Beckett (eds.). *Ulster since 1800, second series: a social survey.* 1957. A series of radio talks.

1019 Mortimer, Roger. *The Jockey Club.* 1958.

1020 Moss, Arthur W. *Valiant crusade: the history of the R.S.P.C.A.* 1961. 150 years of the Royal Society for the Prevention of Cruelty to Animals.

1021 Mowat, Charles L. *The Charity Organisation Society, 1869–1913: its ideas and work.* 1961.

1022 Murphy, James R. *The religious problem in English education: the crucial experiment.* Liverpool, 1959. An important study of the case of Liverpool.

1023 Neff, Wanda F. *Victorian working women: an historical and literary study of women in British industries and professions, 1832–1850.* 1929.

1024 Newman, George. *The building of a nation's health.* 1939. On the public health movement.

1025 Newsome, David. *A history of Wellington College, 1859–1959.* 1959.

1026 Ogilvie, Vivian. *The English public school.* 1957.

1027 Olsen, Donald J. *Town planning in London. The eighteenth and nineteenth centuries.* 1964. A study of the Bedford estate.

1028 Owen, David. *English philanthropy, 1660–1960.* Cambridge, Mass., 1964. A major study.

1029 Pimlott, John A. R. *The Englishman's holiday: a social history.* 1947.

1030 Pinchbeck, Ivy. *Women workers and the industrial revolution, 1750–1850.* 1930.

1031 Polanyi, Karoly. *Origins of our time: the great transformation.* 1945. An anthropological approach to economic and social history.

1032 Prebble, John. *The highland clearances.* 1963.

1033 Pritchard, David G. *Education and the handicapped, 1760–1960.* 1963.

1034 Quennell, Peter. *Victorian panorama, a survey of life and fashion from contemporary photographs.* 1937. Photographs and commentary.

1035 Read, Donald. *The English provinces, c. 1760–1960: a study in influence.* 1964.

1036 Reader, William J. *Professional men; the rise of the professional classes in 19th century England.* 1967. An important history of the professions.

1037 Redford, Arthur. *Labour migration in England 1800–1850,* ed. William H. Chaloner. Rev. ed., Manchester, 1964. Originally published 1926.

1038 Roe, F. Gordon. *The Victorian child.* 1959.

1039 —— *Victorian furniture.* 1952.

1040 Rose, Millicent. *The east end of London.* 1951. A broadly based urban history.

1041 Rowntree, B. Seebohm. *Poverty: a study of town life.* New ed., 1922. A classic social survey of York, originally published 1902.

1042 Salaman, Redcliffe N. *The history and social influence of the potato.* Cambridge, 1949. A remarkable contribution by a botanist.

1043 Saville, John. *Rural depopulation in England and Wales, 1851–1951.* 1957.
1044 Schrier, Arnold. *Ireland and the American emigration, 1850–1900.* Minneapolis, 1958.
1045 Seymer, Lucy R. *Florence Nightingale's nurses: the Nightingale Training School, 1860–1960.* 1960.
1046 Shepperson, Wilbur S. *British emigration to North America: projects and opinions in the early Victorian period.* Oxford, 1957.
1047 Shryock, Richard H. *The history of nursing.* Philadelphia, 1959.
1048 Simey, Margaret B. *Charitable effort in Liverpool in the nineteenth century.* Liverpool, 1951. A model local study.
1049 Simon, Brian. *Education and the labour movement, 1870–1920: studies in the history of education.* 1965.
1050 —— *Studies in the history of education, 1780–1870.* 1960. A useful Marxist approach to the subject.
1051 Simpson, John B. Hope. *Rugby since Arnold: a history of Rugby School from 1842.* 1967.
1052 Smith, Frank. *History of English elementary education 1760–1902.* 1931.
1053 Stafford, Ann [pseud. of Ann Pedler]. *The age of consent.* 1964. On the trial of W. T. Stead, 1885.
1054 Stern, Walter M. *The porters of London.* 1960.
1055 Stewart, W. A. C. and W. P. McCann. *The educational innovators.* 1967, 2 vols.
1056 Sturt, Mary. *The education of the people. A history of primary education in England and Wales in the nineteenth century.* 1967. An important recent study.
1057 Symonds, Robert W. and Bruce B. Whineray. *Victorian furniture.* 1962.
1058 Terrot, Charles. *The maiden tribute.* 1959. On white slavery.
1059 Thompson, Francis M. L. *English landed society in the nineteenth century.* 1963. An important survey.
1060 Thompson, Paul (ed.). *The Victorian poor.* 1967. A symposium.
1061 Thornton, Archibald P. *The habit of authority: paternalism in British history.* Toronto, 1966. A brilliant extended essay.
1062 Thwaite, Mary F. *From primer to pleasure.* 1963. On children's books.
1063 Tobias, John J. *Crime and industrial society in the nineteenth century.* New York, 1967.
1064 Tropp, Asher. *The school teachers: the growth of the teaching profession in England and Wales from 1800 to the present day.* 1957.
1065 Turner, Ernest S. *Call the doctor: a social history of medical men.* 1958.
1066 —— *Roads to ruin; the shocking history of social reform.* 1950. Ten reform movements.
1067 —— *What the butler saw: two hundred and fifty years of the servant problem.* 1962.
1068 Tylecote, Mabel. *The Mechanics' Institutes of Lancashire and Yorkshire before 1851.* Manchester, 1957.
1069 Waterhouse, Rachel E. *Children in hospital: a hundred years of child care in Birmingham.* 1962.
1070 Webb, Robert K. *The British working class reader, 1790–1848: literary and social tensions.* 1955. An illuminating study of literature for the lower classes.
1071 Weber, Adna F. *The growth of cities in the nineteenth century.* 1899. Reprinted, Ithaca, N.Y., 1963. The classic of urban history.
1072 Webster, Frederick A. M. *Our great public schools: their traditions, customs and games.* 1937. Somewhat popular.
1073 West, E. G. *Education and the state: a study in political economy.* 1965.
1074 Wilkinson, John F. *The friendly society movement, its origin, rise, and growth; its social, moral, and educational influences.* 1886.
1075 Wilkinson, Rupert. *The prefects: British leadership and the public school tradition: a comparative study in the making of rulers.* 1964.
1076 Wingfield-Stratford, Esmé C. *The squire and his relations.* 1956. A social history of the gentry.
1077 —— *The Victorian sunset.* 1932. A critical social history of the late Victorians.

1078   Wingfield-Stratford, Esmé C. *The Victorian tragedy.* 1930. American title: *Those earnest Victorians.* Debunking, somewhat in the manner of Lytton Strachey.

1079   Wood, Ethel M. *The Polytechnic of Quintin Hogg.* 1936. A revision of *Quintin Hogg: a biography.* 1932.

1080   Woodham-Smith, Cecil. *The great hunger: Ireland, 1845–49.* 1962. A moving and indignant critique of English policy.

1081   Woodroofe, Kathleen. *From charity to social work in England and the United States.* 1962. The growth of the social work profession.

1082   Wright, Lawrence. *Clean and decent: the fascinating history of the bathroom and the water closet.* 1960. Fascinating indeed.

1083   Wrigley, Edward A. (ed.). *An introduction to English historical demography from the 16th to the 19th century.* 1966.

1084   Young, Agnes F. and Elwyn T. Ashton. *British social work in the nineteenth century.* 1956.

4   Biographies

1085   Battiscombe, Georgina. *Mrs. Gladstone: the portrait of a marriage.* 1956.
1086   Bell, Enid. *Josephine Butler: flame of fire.* 1962.
1087   Butler, Arthur S. G. *Portrait of Josephine Butler.* 1954.
1088   Deacon, Richard. *The private life of Mr. Gladstone.* 1965.
1089   Duff, David. *The shy princess: the life of Her Royal Highness Princess Beatrice, the youngest daughter and constant companion of Queen Victoria.* 1958.

1090   Forster, Edward M. *Marianne Thornton, a domestic biography, 1797–1887.* 1956. An elegant life of a member of the Clapham Sect.

1091   Goldsmith, Margaret. *Florence Nightingale.* 1937.
1092   Harrison, John F. C. *Social reform in Victorian Leeds: the work of James Hole 1820–1895.* Leeds, 1954.

1093   Hewett, Osbert W. *Strawberry fair: a biography of Frances, Countess Waldegrave, 1821–1879.* 1956. Life of a leading London hostess.

1094   Hogg, Ethel. *Quintin Hogg, a biography.* 1904.
1095   Huxley, Gervas. *Victorian duke: the life of Hugh Lupus Grosvenor, first Duke of Westminster.* 1967.

1096   Kamm, Josephine. *How different from us: a biography of Miss Buss and Miss Beale.* New ed., 1958. Lives of two leaders in girls' education.

1097   Londonderry, Edith, Marchioness of. *Frances Anne. The life and times of Frances Anne, Marchioness of Londonderry and her husband, Charles, third Marquess of Londonderry.* 1958.

1098   Morris, Helen. *Portrait of a chef: the life of Alexis Soyer, sometime chef of the Reform Club.* Cambridge, 1938.

1099   Morton, Frederic. *The Rothschilds.* 1962.
1100   Parkin, George R. *Edward Thring, headmaster of Uppingham School; life, diary and letters.* 1898, 2 vols.

1101   Purcell, William. *Onward Christian soldier: a life of Sabine Baring-Gould, parson, squire, novelist, antiquary, 1834–1924.* 1957.

1102   Tisdall, Evelyn E. P. *Queen Victoria's private life, 1837–1901.* 1961.
1103   Wake, Joan. *The Brudenells of Deane.* 2nd ed., 1954. On the Earls of Cardigan.

1104   Woodham-Smith, Cecil. *Florence Nightingale, 1820–1910.* 1950. Important and controversial; see the critique by W. H. Greenleaf, *VS,* **3** (Dec. 1959), 190–202.

5   Articles

(See also sec. VIII, pt. 5, and sec. XII, pt. 5, below.)

1105   Armytage, Walter H. G. 'John Minter Morgan's schemes, 1841–1855', *IRSH,* **3** (pt. 1, 1958), 26–42. Co-operative villages under Church influence.

1106   Banks, Joseph A. 'Population change and the Victorian city', *VS,* **11** (Mar. 1968), 277–89.

1107 Beck, Ann F. 'Issues in the anti-vaccination movement in England', *Medical History*, 4 (Oct. 1960), 310–21.

1108 Bedarida, François. 'L'histoire sociale de Londres au XIXe siècle', *Annales*, 15 (Sept.–Oct. 1960), 949–62.

1109 Best, Geoffrey F. A. 'The road to Hiram's Hospital: a byway of early Victorian history', *VS*, 5 (Dec. 1961), 135–50. On the reform of Church charities.

1110 —— 'The Scottish Victorian city', *VS*, 11 (Mar. 1968), 329–58.

1111 Blanco, Richard L. 'Educational reforms for the enlisted man in the army of Victorian England', *History of Education Quarterly*, 6 (Summer 1966), 61–72.

1112 Booth, Charles. 'Occupations of the people of the United Kingdom, 1801–81', *Journal of the Royal Statistical Society*, 49 (June 1886), 314–435.

1113 Burn, William L. 'Newcastle upon Tyne in the early nineteenth century', *Archaeologia Aeliana*, 4th ser., 34 (1937), 1–13.

1114 Cairncross, Alexander K. 'Internal migration in Victorian England', *Manchester School of Economic and Social Studies*, 17 (Jan. 1949), 67–87.

1115 Cannan, Edwin. 'The changed outlook in regard to population, 1831–1931', *Economic Journal*, 41 (Dec. 1931), 519–33.

1116 Checkland, Sydney G. 'The British industrial city as history: the Glasgow case', *Urban Studies*, 1 (May 1964), 34–54.

1117 Clements, Roger V. 'Trade unions and emigration, 1840–80', *Population Studies*, 9 (Nov. 1955), 167–80.

1118 Cominos, Peter T. 'Late-Victorian sexual respectability and the social system', *IRSH*, 8 (pts. 1–2, 1963), 18–48, 216–50. A seminal article.

1119 Connell, Kenneth H. 'Land legislation and Irish social life', *EcHR*, 2nd ser., 11 (Aug. 1958), 1–7.

1120 —— 'Peasant marriage in Ireland: its structure and development since the famine', *EcHR*, 2nd ser., 14 (Apr. 1962), 502–23. Important.

1121 —— 'Some unsettled problems in English and Irish population history', *IHS*, 7 (Sept. 1951), 225–34.

1122 Cousens, S. H. 'Emigration and demographic change in Ireland, 1851–1861', *EcHR*, 2nd ser., 14 (Dec. 1961), 275–88.

1123 Cruickshank, Marjorie. 'The Argyll Commission report, 1865–8: a landmark in Scottish education', *British Journal of Educational Studies*, 15 (June 1967), 133–47.

1124 Dyos, Harold J. 'Railways and housing in Victorian England', *Journal of Transport History*, 2 (no. 2, 1956), 90–100.

1125 —— 'Railways and the effect their building had on housing in Victorian London', *Journal of Transport History*, 2 (no. 1, 1955), 11–21.

1126 —— 'The slums of Victorian London', *VS*, 11 (Sept. 1967), 5–40.

1127 Erickson, Charlotte. 'The encouragement of emigration by British trade unions, 1850–1900', *Population Studies*, 3 (Dec. 1949), 248–73.

1128 Fein, Albert. 'Victoria Park: its origin and history', *East London Papers*, 5 (Oct. 1962), 73–90.

1129 Frangopulo, Nicholas J. 'Foreign communities in Victorian Manchester', *Manchester Review*, 10 (Spring–Summer 1965), 189–206.

1130 Fulford, Roger. 'Victorian and Edwardian London', in Arnold Toynbee (ed.). *Cities of destiny*. 1967, pp. 276–95. Illustrated.

1131 Glass, David V. 'Changes in fertility in England and Wales, 1851 to 1931', in Lancelot Hogben (ed.). *Political arithmetic, a symposium of population studies*. 1938, pp. 161–212.

1132 Harrison, Brian. 'Philanthropy and the Victorians', *VS*, 9 (June 1966), 353–74.

1133 Harrison, John F. C. 'The Victorian gospel of success', *VS*, 1 (Dec. 1957), 155–64.

1134 Heasman, Kathleen J. 'The medical mission and the care of the sick poor in nineteenth-century England', *Hist.J.*, 7 (no. 2, 1964), 230–45.

1135 Heath, Frederick B. 'The Grenvilles in the nineteenth century: the emergence of commercial affiliations', *Huntington Library Quarterly*, 25 (Nov. 1961), 29–49.

1136 Hollingsworth, Thomas H. 'A demographic study of the British ducal families', *Population Studies*, **11** (July 1957), 4–26.

1137 Holloway, S. W. F. 'Medical education in England, 1830–1858: a socio-logical analysis', *History*, **49** (Oct. 1964), 299–324.

1138 Jenkins, Hester and D. Caradog Jones. 'Social class of Cambridge University alumni of the 18th and 19th centuries', *British Journal of Sociology*, **1** (June 1950), 93–116.

1139 Krause, John T. 'Changes in English fertility and mortality, 1781–1850', *EcHR*, 2nd ser., **11** (Aug. 1958), 52–70. A very careful study.

1140 Logan, William P. D. 'Mortality in England and Wales from 1848 to 1947', *Population Studies*, **4** (Sept. 1951), 132–78. Surveys the changing causes of death. ✓

1141 MacDonagh, Oliver. 'The Irish Catholic clergy and emigration during the great famine', *IHS*, **5** (Sept. 1947), 287–302.

1142 MacDonald, Robert H. 'The frightful consequences of onanism: notes on the history of a delusion', *JHI*, **28** (July 1967), 423–31.

1143 McGregor, Oliver R. 'Social research and social policy in the nineteenth century', *British Journal of Sociology*, **8** (June 1957), 146–57. ✓

1144 McKeown, Thomas and Record, R. G. 'Reasons for the decline of mortality in England and Wales during the nineteenth century', *Population Studies*, **16** (Nov. 1962), 94–122.

1145 MacLeod, Roy M. 'The edge of hope: social policy and chronic alcoholism 1870–1900', *Journal of the History of Medicine*, **22** (July 1967), 215–45.

1146 Marshall, Thomas H. 'The population of England and Wales from the industrial revolution to the World War', in *Ess. Ec. Hist.*, I, 331–43.

1147 Moore, D. Cresap. 'Social structure, political structure, and public opinion in mid-Victorian England', in *Id. & Inst.*, pp. 20–57.

1148 Musgrave, P. W. 'Constant factors in the demand for technical education: 1860–1960', *British Journal of Educational Studies*, **14** (May 1966), 173–87.

1149 Musgrove, Frank. 'Middle-class education and employment in the nineteenth century', *EcHR*, 2nd ser., **12** (Aug. 1959), 99–111. See the 'critical note' by Harold J. Perkin, *ibid.*, **14** (Aug. 1961), 122–30, and Musgrove's 'rejoinder', *ibid.* (Dec. 1961), 320–9.

1150 O'Neill, James E. 'Finding a policy for the sick poor', *VS*, **7** (Mar. 1964), 265–84. Covers the period from 1834 to the 1860s.

1151 Owen, David. 'The city parochial charities: the "dead hand" in late Victorian London', *JBS*, **1** (May 1962), 115–35.

1152 Pumphrey, Ralph E. 'The introduction of industrialists into the British peerage; a study in adaptation of a social institution', *AHR*, **65** (Oct. 1959), 1–16.

1153 Ravetz, Alison. 'The Victorian coal kitchen and its reformers', *VS*, **11** (June 1968), 435–60.

1154 Selleck, R. J. W. 'The scientific educationist, 1870–1914', *British Journal of Educational Studies*, **15** (June 1967), 148–65.

1155 Shannon, Herbert A. 'Migration and the growth of London, 1841–91, a statistical note', *EcHR*, **5** (Apr. 1935), 79–86.

1156 Soffer, R. N. 'Attitudes and allegiances of the unskilled North, 1830–1850', *IRSH*, **10** (pt. 3, 1965), 429–54.

1157 Spring, David. 'Aristocracy, social structure, and religion in the early Victorian period', *VS*, **6** (Mar. 1963), 263–80.

1158 —— 'The role of the aristocracy in the late nineteenth century', *VS*, **4** (Sept. 1960), 55–64.

1159 Spring, David and Eileen. 'The fall of the Grenvilles, 1844–1848', *Huntington Library Quarterly*, **19** (Feb. 1956), 165–90. On the ruin of the Duke of Buckingham and Chandos.

1160 Stansky, Peter L. 'Lyttelton and Thring: a study in nineteenth-century education', *VS*, **5** (Mar. 1962), 205–23.

1161 Tarn, John N. 'The Peabody donation fund: the role of a housing society in the nineteenth century', *VS*, **10** (Sept. 1966), 7–38.

1162 Taylor, Arthur J. 'Progress and poverty in Britain, 1780–1850: a re-appraisal', in *Ess. Ec. Hist.*, III, 380–93. Summarizes the debate over the effects of the industrial revolution.

1163 Thompson, Edward P. 'The political education of Henry Mayhew', *VS*, 11 (Sept. 1967), 41–62. The background of (872).

1164 Webb, Robert K. 'Literacy among the working classes in nineteenth century Scotland', *SHR*, 33 (Dec. 1955), 100–14.

1165 —— 'Working class readers in early Victorian England', *EHR*, 65 (July 1950), 333–51.

1166 Welton, Thomas A. 'On the distribution of population in England and Wales, and its progress in the period of ninety years from 1801 to 1891', *Journal of the Royal Statistical Society*, 63 (Dec. 1900), 527–89.

1167 Wilkinson, Rupert. 'Political leadership and the late Victorian public school', *British Journal of Sociology*, 13 (Dec. 1962), 320–30. Argues that the real purpose of the public schools was the preparation of capable public servants.

VIII ECONOMIC HISTORY

1 Printed sources

1168 *Abstract of labour statistics*. 1889–. Published annually by the Board of Trade.

1169 Cole, George D. H. and Alexander W. Filson (eds.). *British working class movements: select documents, 1789–1875.* 1951.

1170 Court, William H. B. (ed.). *British economic history, 1870–1914: commentary and documents.* Cambridge, 1965.

1171 *Directory of directors . . . List of the directors of all the principal companies of the United Kingdom . . . and of their other business connections, 1880–.* 1880–. Annual.

1172 Elsas, Madeleine (ed.). *Iron in the making: Dowlais Iron Company letters, 1782–1860.* Cardiff, 1960.

1173 Gregory, Theodore E. G. (ed.). *Select statutes, documents and reports relating to British banking 1832–1928.* 1929, 2 vols.

1174 Jefferys, James B. (ed.). *Labour's formative years, 1849–1879.* 1948.

1175 Mann, Tom. *Tom Mann's memoirs.* 1923. Useful for labour history.

1176 Mitchell, Brian R., with Phyllis Deane. *Abstract of British historical statistics.* Cambridge, 1962. A basic reference work, with text explaining the sources.

1177 Mulhall, Michael G. *Dictionary of statistics.* 4th ed., 1899. See also (continuing from Nov. 1898), Augustus D. Webb. *The new dictionary of statistics.* 1911.

1178 Page, William (ed.). *Commerce and industry*, I, *A historical review of the economic conditions of the British Empire from the peace of Paris in 1815 to the declaration of war in 1914, based on parliamentary debates*, II, *Tables of statistics for the British Empire from 1815.* 1919, 2 vols.

1179 *Reports of the annual Trades Union Congress.* Manchester, 1870–.

1180 *Statistical abstract of the United Kingdom.* 1854–. In *Parliamentary papers.*

1181 Sturt, George. *The wheelwright's shop.* Cambridge, 1923. Reminiscences of the transformation of an old craft.

2 Surveys
(See also sec. VII, pt. 2, above.)

1182 Ashworth, William. *An economic history of England, 1870–1939.* 1960. A reliable survey.

1183 Brentano, Lujo. *Eine Geschichte der wirtschaftlichen Entwicklung Englands.* Jena, 1927–9, 3 vols.

1184 Chambers, Jonathan D. *The workshop of the world: British economic history from 1820 to 1880.* 1961.

1185 Clapham, John H. *An economic history of modern Britain.* 2nd ed., Cambridge, 1950–2, 3 vols. A massive but readable monument of scholarship, covering the period 1820–1929.

1186 Court, William H. B. *A concise economic history of Britain from 1750 to recent times.* Cambridge, 1954. The best brief survey.

1187 Cunningham, William. *The growth of English industry and commerce,* II. 5th ed., Cambridge, 1912.

1188 Deane, Phyllis. *The first industrial revolution.* Cambridge, 1965. Covers 1750–1850.

1189 Derry, Thomas K. and Thomas L. Jarman. *The making of modern Britain: life and work from George III to Elizabeth II.* 1956.

1190 Fay, Charles R. *Great Britain from Adam Smith to the present day.* 2nd ed., 1950.

1191 Gayer, Arthur D., Walt W. Rostow and Anna J. Schwartz. *The growth and fluctuation of the British economy, 1790–1850: an historical, statistical and theoretical study of Britain's economic development.* Oxford, 1953, 2 vols. An important quantitative study.

1192 Habakkuk, Hrothgar J. and Michael M. Postan (eds.). *The Cambridge economic history of Europe,* VI, *The industrial revolutions and after: incomes, population, and technological change.* Cambridge, 1965, 1 vol. in 2.

1193 Hammond, John L. and Barbara. *The rise of modern industry.* 5th ed., 1937. A Fabian approach.

1194 Knowles, Lillian C. A. *The industrial and commercial revolutions in Great Britain during the nineteenth century.* 4th ed., 1926.

1195 Pool, Arthur G. and Gwilym P. Jones. *A hundred years of economic development in Great Britain.* 1940.

1196 Redford, Arthur. *The economic history of England, 1760–1860.* 2nd ed., 1960.

1197 Rostow, Walt W. *The British economy of the nineteenth century.* Oxford, 1948. Useful and suggestive. For a critique (on the issue of whether real wages rose), see John Saville. 'A comment on Professor Rostow's *British economy of the nineteenth century*', *PP,* **6** (Nov. 1954), 66–81.

1198 Slater, Gilbert. *The growth of modern England.* 2nd ed., 1939.

3 Monographs

(See also sec. VII, pt. 3, above.)

1199 Acres, W. Marston. *The Bank of England from within, 1694–1900.* 1931, 2 vols.

1200 Acworth, William M. *The railways of England.* 5th ed., 1900. Casual essays, but rich in material.

1201 Addis, John P. *The Crawshay dynasty: a study in industrial organisation and development.* Cardiff, 1957. A good study of an iron firm.

1202 Aldcroft, Derek H. (ed.). *The development of British industry and foreign competition, 1875–1914: studies in industrial enterprise.* Glasgow, 1968.

1203 Allen, George C. *The industrial development of Birmingham and the Black Country, 1860–1927.* 1929.

1204 Andreades, Andreas M. *History of the Bank of England,* tr. Christabel Meredith. 1909.

1205 Armitage, Godfrey W. *The Lancashire cotton industry from the great inventions to the great disaster.* Manchester, 1951.

1206 Arnot, Robert P. *The miners; a history of the Miners' Federation of Great Britain, 1889–1910.* 1949.

1207 Bagwell, Philip. *The railwaymen: the history of the National Union of Railwaymen.* 1963.

1208 Bailey, Jack. *The British co-operative movement.* 1955.

1209 Barker, Theodore C. *Pilkington Brothers and the glass industry.* 1960. A model business history.

1210 Barker, Theodore C. and Michael Robbins. *A history of London transport; passenger travel and the development of the metropolis,* I, *The nineteenth century.* 1963.

1211 Barnes, Eric G. *The rise of the Midland Railway, 1844–1874.* 1966.
1212 Barnes, James J. *Free trade in books: a study of the London book trade since 1800.* Oxford, 1964.
1213 Bowley, Arthur L. *The change in the distribution of the national income 1880–1913.* Oxford, 1920.
1214 —— *Wages and income in the United Kingdom since 1860.* Cambridge, 1937.
1215 Brentano, Lujo. *On the history and development of gilds, and the origin of trade unions.* 1870. The first major work in labour history.
1216 Briggs, Asa and John Saville (eds.). *Essays in labour history, in memory of G. D. H. Cole.* 1960. An important collection.
1217 Buckley, Kenneth D. *Trade unionism in Aberdeen, 1878 to 1900.* Edinburgh, 1955.
1218 Burn, Duncan L. *The economic history of steelmaking 1867–1939; a study in competition.* Cambridge, 1940.
1219 Burnham, Thomas H. and George O. Hoskins. *Iron and steel in Britain, 1870–1930. A comparative study of the causes which limited the economic development of the British iron and steel industry between the years 1870 and 1930.* 1943.
1220 Cairncross, Alexander K. *Home and foreign investment, 1870–1913: studies in capital accumulation.* Cambridge, 1953.
1221 Cannan, Edwin. *The history of local rates in England, in relation to the proper distribution of the burden of taxation.* 2nd ed., 1912.
1222 Carr, James C. and Walter Taplin. *History of the British steel industry.* Oxford, 1962.
1223 Carr-Saunders, Alexander M., P. Sargent Florence and Robert Peers. *Consumers' co-operation in Great Britain.* 1938.
1224 Carter, Ernest F. *An historical geography of the railways of the British Isles.* 1959.
1225 Chandler, Dean and A. Douglas Lacey. *The rise of the gas industry in Britain.* 1949.
1226 Chandler, George. *Liverpool shipping: a short history.* 1960.
1227 Chapman, Sidney J. *The Lancashire cotton industry: a study in economic development.* Manchester, 1904.
1228 Church, Roy A. *Economic and social change in a midland town: Victorian Nottingham, 1815–1900.* 1966.
1229 Clair, Colin. *A history of printing in Britain.* 1966.
1230 Clapham, John H. *The Bank of England: a history, 1694–1914,* II. Cambridge, 1944. The standard work.
1231 —— *The woollen and worsted industries.* 1907.
1232 Clark, Edwin A. C. *The ports of the Exe estuary: 1660–1860; a study in historical geography.* Exeter, 1960.
1233 Clegg, Hugh A. C., Alan Fox and Arthur F. Thompson. *A history of British trade unions since 1889,* I. Oxford, 1964. Encyclopaedic.
1234 Cole, George D. H. *A century of co-operation.* 1944.
1235 —— *Short history of the English working class movement, 1789–1947.* 2nd ed., 1948. A good Fabian account.
1236 Coleman, Donald C. *The British paper industry, 1495–1860: a study in industrial growth.* Oxford, 1958.
1237 Corbett, John. *The Birmingham Trades Council, 1866–1966.* 1966.
1238 Cornewall-Jones, R. J. *The British merchant service; being a history of the British mercantile marine from the earliest times to the present day.* 1898.
1239 Corry, Bernard A. *Money, saving, and investment in English economics, 1800–1850.* 1962.
1240 Cramp, Alfred B. *Opinion on bank rate, 1822–60.* 1962.
1241 Crick, Wilfred F. and John E. Wadsworth. *A hundred years of joint stock banking.* 1936.
1242 Critchell, James T. and Joseph Raymond. *A history of the frozen meat trade; an account of the development and present day methods of preparation, transport, and marketing of frozen and chilled meats.* 1912.
1243 Day, John R. *The story of London's Underground.* Rev. ed., 1966.

42

1244 Deane, Phyllis and William A. Cole. *British economic growth, 1688–1959, trends and structure.* Cambridge, 1962. A major study.

1245 Dickson, Peter G. M. *The Sun Insurance Office, 1710–1960: the history of two and a half centuries of British insurance.* 1960.

1246 Dodd, Arthur H. *The industrial revolution in North Wales.* 2nd ed., Cardiff, 1951.

1247 Dowell, Stephen. *A history of taxation and taxes in England from the earliest times to the year 1885,* II–IV. 2nd ed., 1888.

1248 Edwards, Harold R. *Competition and monopoly in the British soap industry.* Oxford, 1962.

1249 Elliott, Blanche B. *A history of English advertising.* 1962.

1250 Ellis, C. Hamilton. *British railway history: an outline from the accession of William IV to the nationalisation of railways.* 1954–9, 2 vols. Ellis is also the author of numerous monographs on particular railways and on railway equipment.

1251 Emden, Paul H. *Money powers of Europe in the nineteenth and twentieth centuries.* 1937. Deals with financiers and banking houses.

1252 Erickson, Charlotte. *British industrialists: steel and hosiery: 1850–1950.* Cambridge, 1959. A sociological comparison of the personnel of two industries.

1253 Evans, Eric W. *The miners of South Wales.* Cardiff, 1961.

1254 Eyles, Desmond. *Royal Doulton, 1815–1965: the rise and expansion of the Royal Doulton potteries.* 1965.

1255 Fay, Charles R. (ed.). *Round about industrial Britain, 1830–1860.* 1952. A series of lectures.

1256 Feavearyear, Albert E. *The pound sterling: a history of English money,* rev. by E. Victor Morgan. 2nd ed., 1963.

1257 Flanders, Allen and Hugh A. Clegg. *The system of industrial relations in Great Britain: its history, law and institutions.* Oxford, 1954.

1258 Ford, Alec G. *The gold standard 1880–1914: Britain and Argentina.* Oxford, 1962.

1259 Fox, Alan. *A history of the National Union of Boot and Shoe Operatives, 1874–1957.* Oxford, 1958.

1260 Gibbs, Charles R. V. *British passenger liners of the five oceans: a record of the British passenger lines and their liners from 1838 to the present day.* 1963.

1261 Gosden, Peter H. J. H. *The friendly societies in England, 1815–1875.* Manchester, 1961.

1262 Gregory, Theodore E. G., assisted by Annette Henderson. *The Westminster Bank through a century.* 1936, 2 vols.

1263 Grinling, Charles H. *The history of the Great Northern Railway, 1845–1922,* with additional chapters by H. V. Borley and C. Hamilton Ellis. 2nd ed., 1967. Originally published 1898.

1264 Haber, Ludwig F. *The chemical industry during the nineteenth century: a study of the economic aspect of applied chemistry in Europe and North America.* Oxford, 1958. An important study.

1265 Hall, Fred and William P. Watkins. *Co-operation: a survey of the history, principles and organization of the co-operative movement in Great Britain and Ireland.* Manchester, 1934.

1266 Hall, Peter G. *The industries of London since 1861.* 1962.

1267 Handover, Phyllis M. *Printing in London from 1476 to modern times.* 1960. Economic and technical developments in printing.

1268 Hargreaves, Eric L. *The national debt.* 1930.

1269 Henderson, William O. *Britain and industrial Europe, 1750–1870.* Liverpool, 1954.

1270 —— *The Lancashire cotton famine, 1861–1865.* Manchester, 1934.

1271 Hidy, Ralph. *The house of Baring in American trade and finance, 1763–1861.* Cambridge, Mass., 1949.

1272 Hilton, George W. *The truck system: including a history of the British Truck Acts, 1465–1960.* 1961.

1273 Hilton, William S. *Foes to tyranny: a history of the Amalgamated Union of Building Trade Workers.* 1963.

1274 Hirst, Francis W. *Gladstone as financier and economist.* 1931.
1275 —— *The Stock Exchange: a short study of investment and speculation.* 1911.
1276 Hoffman, Ross J. *Great Britain and the German trade rivalry.* Philadelphia, 1933.
1277 Hoffmann, Walther G. *British industry, 1700–1950,* tr. William O. Henderson and William H. Chaloner. Oxford, 1955. Highly technical.
1278 —— *The growth of industrial economics,* tr. William O. Henderson and William H. Chaloner. Manchester, 1958.
1279 Holyoake, George J. *History of co-operation in England.* Rev. ed., 1906, 2 vols.
1280 Horne, H. Oliver. *A history of savings banks.* Oxford, 1947.
1281 Howe, Ellic and John Child. *The Society of London Bookbinders, 1780–1951.* 1952. A trade union history.
1282 Hughes, Jonathan R. T. *Fluctuations in trade, industry and finance: a study of British economic development 1850–1860.* 1960.
1283 Hunt, Bishop C. *The development of the business corporation in England 1800–1867.* Cambridge, Mass., 1936.
1284 Hutchison, Keith. *The decline and fall of British capitalism.* 2nd ed., 1967. A useful journalistic study of the period since 1880.
1285 Hyde, Francis E., with John R. Harris and A. M. Bourne. *Shipping enterprise and management 1830–1939: Harrisons of Liverpool.* Liverpool, 1967. A good business history of a steamship company.
1286 Hyde, Francis E., with John R. Harris. *Blue funnel: a history of Alfred Holt and Company of Liverpool from 1865 to 1914.* Liverpool, 1956.
1287 Ilersic, Alfred R. and Patricia F. B. Liddle. *Parliament of commerce: the story of the Association of British Chambers of Commerce 1860–1960.* 1960. Interesting on the relationship between business and government.
1288 Imlah, Albert H. *Economic elements in the Pax Britannica: studies in British foreign trade in the nineteenth century.* Cambridge, Mass., 1958. A valuable study.
1289 Jackman, William T. *The development of transportation in modern England.* 2nd ed., 1962, 2 vols. The standard work.
1290 Jefferys, James B. *Retail trading in Britain 1850–1950: a study of trends in retailing with special reference to the development of co-operative, multiple shop and department store methods of trading.* Cambridge, 1954.
1291 —— *The story of the engineers, 1800–1945.* 1946. A competent trade union history.
1292 Jenks, Leland H. *The migration of British capital to 1875.* 1927.
1293 John, Arthur H. *The industrial development of South Wales, 1750–1850; an essay.* Cardiff, 1950.
1294 —— *A Liverpool merchant house; being the history of Alfred Booth and Company, 1863–1958.* 1959.
1295 Kindleberger, Charles P. *Economic growth in France and Britain, 1851–1950.* Cambridge, Mass., 1964.
1296 King, Wilfred T. C. *History of the London discount market.* 1936.
1297 Kirkaldy, Adam W. *British shipping, its history, organisation, and importance.* 1914.
1298 Kuczynski, Jürgen. *Darstellung der Lage der Arbeiter in England: von 1832 bis 1900.* Berlin, 1964.
1299 Layton, Walter T. and Geoffrey Crowther. *An introduction to the history of prices, with special reference to the history of the nineteenth century.* 3rd ed., 1938.
1300 Leighton-Boyce, John A. S. L. *Smiths the bankers, 1658–1958.* 1958.
1301 Levine, Aaron L. *Industrial retardation in Britain, 1880–1914.* New York, 1967.
1302 Lewis, J. Parry. *Building cycles and Britain's growth.* 1965.
1303 Lindsay, William S. *History of merchant shipping and ancient commerce,* IV. 1876. Still useful.
1304 Lloyd, Godfrey I. H. *The cutlery trades: an historical essay in the economics of small-scale production.* 1913.
1305 Lynch, Patrick and John Vaizey. *Guinness's brewery in the Irish economy, 1759–1876.* Cambridge, 1960.

1306 MacDermot, Edward T. *History of the Great Western Railway*. Rev. ed., 1967, 3 vols.
1307 Machin, Frank. *The Yorkshire miners: a history*. Barnsley, 1958.
1308 Mallett, Bernard. *British budgets, 1887–88 to 1912–13*. 1913. Analyses of each budget.
1309 Marriner, Sheila. *Rathbones of Liverpool 1845–73*. Liverpool, 1961.
1310 Marshall, John D. *Furness and the industrial revolution: an economic history of Furness (1711–1900) and the town of Barrow (1757–1897)*. Barrow-in-Furness, 1958. A regional study, important for the steel industry.
1311 Marwick, William H. *Economic developments in Victorian Scotland*. 1936.
1312 —— *Scottish labour*. Glasgow, 1949. A brief summary.
1313 Mathias, Peter. *Retailing revolution*. 1967. On Lipton and the rise of supermarkets.
1314 Matthews, Philip W. *History of Barclays Bank, Limited, including the many private and joint stock banks amalgamated and affiliated with it*, ed. Anthony W. Tuke. 1926.
1315 Matthews, Robert C. O. *A study in trade-cycle history: economic fluctuations in Great Britain, 1833–1842*. Cambridge, 1954.
1316 Middlebrook, Sydney. *Newcastle upon Tyne, its growth and achievement*. Newcastle upon Tyne, 1950.
1317 Minchinton, Walter E. *The British tinplate industry*. Oxford, 1957. A good history of a small export industry.
1318 Morgan, E. Victor. *The theory and practice of central banking, 1797–1913*. Cambridge, 1943.
1319 Morgan, E. Victor and William A. Thomas. *The Stock Exchange: its history and functions*. 1962.
1320 Morris, John H. and Lawrence J. Williams. *The south Wales coal industry, 1841–1875*. Cardiff, 1958.
1321 Munro, Neil. *The history of the Royal Bank of Scotland, 1727–1927*. Edinburgh, 1928.
1322 Musson, Alfred E. *The Typographical Association; origins and history up to 1949*. 1954. Trade union history.
1323 Nock, Oswald S. *British steam railways*. 1961.
1324 —— *The Great Western Railway in the nineteenth century*. 1962.
1325 —— *Scottish railways*. Rev. ed., 1961. Nock is the author of several other books on railway history.
1326 O'Brien, George A. T. *The economic history of Ireland from the union to the great famine*. Dublin, 1921.
1327 Pasdermadjian, Hrant. *The department store, its origins, evolution and economics*. 1954.
1328 Pelling, Henry. *A history of British trade unionism*. 1963. One of the standard works.
1329 *Perkins centenary, London: 100 years of synthetic dyestuffs*. 1958.
1330 Phelps Brown, Ernest H. *The growth of British industrial relations: a study from the standpoint of 1906–1914*. 1959.
1331 Phelps Brown, Ernest H. and S. V. Hopkins. *The course of wage rates in five countries, 1860–1939*. Oxford, 1950. A comparative study.
1332 Pollard, Sidney. *A history of labour in Sheffield*. Liverpool, 1959. An important study.
1333 Porter, George R. *The progress of the nation, in its various social and economic relations, from the beginning of the nineteenth century*, rev. by Francis W. Hirst. Rev. ed., 1912. A valuable handbook of miscellaneous statistical information on social and economic history.
1334 Postgate, Raymond. *The builders' history*. 1923. A history of the trade union of the builders, carpenters and joiners.
1335 Powell, Ellis T. *The evolution of the money market (1385–1915): an historical and analytical study of the rise and development of finance as a centralised, co-ordinated force*. 1915.
1336 Prest, John. *The industrial revolution in Coventry*. Oxford, 1960. A local study with a broad view.
1337 Price, J. Seymour. *Building societies, their origin and history*. 1958.

1338 Raynes, Harold E. *A history of British insurance.* Rev. ed., 1950.
1339 Redfern, Percy. *The new history of the C.W.S.* 1938. On the Co-operative Wholesale Society.
1340 Redford, Arthur. *Manchester merchants and foreign trade 1850–1939.* Manchester, 1934–56, 2 vols.
1341 Rees, James F. *A short fiscal and financial history of England 1815–1918.* 1921.
1342 Rimmer, William G. *Marshalls of Leeds, flax-spinners, 1788–1886.* Cambridge, 1960.
1343 Rippy, J. Fred. *British investments in Latin America, 1822–1949: a case study in the operations of private enterprise in retarded regions.* Minneapolis, 1959.
1344 Robbins, R. Michael. *The railway age.* 1962.
1345 Roberts, Benjamin C. *The Trades Union Congress, 1868–1921.* 1958. The authoritative study.
1346 Robertson, William A. *Combination among railway companies.* 1912.
1347 Robins, Frederick W. *The story of water supply.* Oxford, 1946.
1348 Robinson, Howard. *Carrying British mails overseas.* New York, 1964.
1349 Sabine, Basil E. V. *A history of income tax.* 1966.
1350 Sauerbeck, Augustus. *The course of average prices of general commodities in England.* 1908. Covers 1815–1907.
1351 Saul, Samuel B. *Studies in British overseas trade, 1870–1914.* Liverpool, 1960. Excellent presentation of an important period.
1352 Savage, Christopher I. *An economic history of transport.* 1959.
1353 Sayers, Richard S. *Central banking after Bagehot.* Oxford, 1957. On the period after 1873.
1354 —— *A history of economic change in England, 1880–1939.* 1967.
1355 —— *Lloyds Bank in the history of English banking.* Oxford, 1957.
1356 Schlote, Werner. *British overseas trade from 1700 to the 1930's,* tr. William O. Henderson and William H. Chaloner. Oxford, 1952. A useful survey.
1357 Scott, John D. *Siemens Brothers, 1858–1958: an essay in the history of industry.* 1958.
1358 —— *Vickers, a history.* 1962.
1359 Sherrington, Charles E. R. *A hundred years of inland transport, 1830–1933.* 1934.
1360 Shihab, Fakhri. *Progressive taxation: a study in the development of the progressive principle in the British income tax.* Oxford, 1953.
1361 Sigsworth, Eric M. *Black Dyke Mills: a history, with introductory chapters on the history of the worsted industry in the nineteenth century.* Liverpool, 1958.
1362 Silver, Arthur W. *Manchester men and Indian cotton, 1847–1872.* Manchester, 1966.
1363 Simmons, Jack. *The railways of Britain: an historical introduction.* 1961.
1364 Stacey, Nicholas A. H. *English accountancy, a study in social and economic history, 1800–1954.* 1954.
1365 Staff, Frank. *The penny post, 1680–1918.* 1964.
1366 Stafford, Ann [pseud. of Ann Pedler]. *A match to fire the Thames.* 1961. On the London dock strike of 1889.
1367 Stamp, Josiah C., Baron. *British incomes and property: the application of official statistics to economic problems.* 1916.
1368 Stirling, Everard. *History of the Gas, Light and Coke Company.* 1949.
1369 Swift, Henry G. *A history of postal agitation from fifty years ago till the present day.* New ed., 1929. Postal workers' unionization, 1850–1900.
1370 Sykes, Joseph. *The amalgamation movement in English banking, 1825–1924.* 1926.
1371 Tate, George (ed.). *London Trades Council, 1860–1950: a history.* 1950.
1372 Taylor, Frank Sherwood. *A history of industrial chemistry.* 1957.
1373 Thomas, Brinley. *Migration and economic growth: a study of Great Britain and the Atlantic economy.* Cambridge, 1954. An important study of the inter-relationship of the British and American economies.
1374 Thomas, David St J. (ed.). *A regional history of the railways of Great Britain.* 1960–6, 4 vols.
1375 Thornton, Roland H. *British shipping.* Cambridge, 1939.

1376 Turnbull, Geoffrey A. *A history of the calico printing industry*. Altrincham, 1951.
1377 Turner, Herbert A. *Trade union growth, structure and policy: a comparative study of the cotton unions*. 1962.
1378 Warren, James G. H. *A century of locomotive building by Robert Stephenson & Co., 1823–1923*. Newcastle, 1923.
1379 Webb, Sidney and Beatrice. *The history of trade unionism*. Rev. ed., 1920. A Fabian classic, now undergoing revision.
1380 Williams, D. Trevor. *The economic development of Swansea and of the Swansea district to 1921*. Swansea, 1940.
1381 Williams, James E. *The Derbyshire miners: a study in industrial and social history*. 1962.
1382 Wilson, Charles H. and William Reader. *Men and machines: a history of D. Napier & Son, Engineers, Ltd., 1808–1958*. 1958.
1383 Withers, Hartley. *The National Provincial Bank, 1833–1933*. 1933.
1384 Wood, Elmer. *English theories of central banking control, 1819–1858, with some account of contemporary procedure*. Cambridge, Mass., 1939.
1385 Woodruff, William. *The rise of the British rubber industry during the nineteenth century*. Liverpool, 1958.

4 Biographies

1386 Clapp, Brian W. *John Owens: Manchester merchant*. Manchester, 1965.
1387 Evans, Eric W. *Mabon: a study in trade union leadership*. Cardiff, 1959. A biography of William Abraham, a leader of the south Wales coal miners.
1388 Humphrey, Arthur W. *Robert Applegarth: trade unionist, educationist, reformer*. 1913.
1389 Lambert, Richard S. *The railway king, 1800–1871: a study of George Hudson and the business morals of his time*. 1934.
1390 Middlemas, Robert K. *The master builders: Thomas Brassey, Sir John Aird, Lord Cowdray, and Sir John Norton-Griffiths*. 1963.
1391 Torr, Dona. *Tom Mann and his times*. 1956. See (1175).
1392 Vernon, Anne. *A Quaker business man: the life of Joseph Rowntree, 1836–1925*. 1958.

5 Articles

1393 Aldcroft, Derek H. 'The entrepreneur and the British economy, 1870–1914', *EcHR*, 2nd ser., **17** (Aug. 1964), 113–34.
1394 —— 'Technical progress and British enterprise, 1875–1914', *Business History*, **8** (July 1966), 122–39.
1395 Alford, B. N. E. 'Business enterprise and the growth of the commercial letterpress printing industry, 1850–1914', *Business History*, **7** (Jan. 1965), 1–14.
1396 —— 'Government expenditure and the growth of the printing industry in the nineteenth century', *EcHR*, 2nd ser., **17** (Aug. 1964), 96–112.
1397 Allen, Victor L. 'The origins of industrial conciliation and arbitration', *IRSH*, **9** (pt. 2, 1964), 237–54.
1398 Anderson, Olive. 'Early experiences of manpower problems in an industrial society at war: Great Britain, 1854–56', *Political Science Quarterly*, **82** (Dec. 1967), 526–45.
1399 —— 'Loans versus taxes: British financial policy in the Crimean war', *EcHR*, 2nd ser., **16** (Dec. 1963), 314–27.
1400 Armstrong, D. L. 'Social and economic conditions in the Belfast linen industry, 1850–1900', *IHS*, **7** (Sept. 1951), 235–69.
1401 Ashworth, William. 'Changes in the industrial structure: 1870–1914', *Yorkshire Bulletin of Economic and Social Research*, **17** (May 1965), 61–74.
1402 —— 'The late Victorian economy', *Economica*, **33** (Feb. 1966), 17–33.
1403 Barker, Theodore C. 'Passenger transport in nineteenth-century London', *Journal of Transport History*, **6** (May 1964), 166–74.

1404 Baxter, R. Dudley. 'Railway extension and its results', in *Ess. Ec. Hist.*, III, 29–67.

1405 Beales, Hugh L. 'The "great depression" in industry and trade', in *Ess. Ec. Hist.*, I, 406–15.

1406 Bellerby, John R. 'National and agricultural income: 1851', *Economic Journal*, **49** (Mar. 1959), 95–104.

1407 Blackman, Janet and Eric M. Sigsworth. 'The house boom of the 1890's', *Yorkshire Bulletin of Economic and Social Research*, **17** (May 1965), 75–97.

1408 Blaug, Mark. 'The productivity of capital in the Lancashire cotton industry during the nineteenth century', *EcHR*, 2nd ser., **13** (Apr. 1961), 358–81.

1409 Brown, Alexander J. Y. 'Britain in the world economy, 1870–1914', *Yorkshire Bulletin of Economic and Social Research*, **17** (May 1965), 46–60.

1410 —— 'Trade union policy in the Scots coalfields, 1855–1885', *EcHR*, 2nd ser., **6** (Aug. 1953), 35–50.

1411 Butt, John. 'Technical change and the growth of the British shale-oil industry (1680–1870)', *EcHR*, 2nd ser., **17** (Apr. 1965), 511–21.

1412 Cairncross, Alexander K. and Bernard Weber. 'Fluctuations in building in Great Britain, 1785–1849', in *Ess. Ec. Hist.*, III, 318–33.

1413 Church, Roy A. and Barbara M. D. Smith. 'Competition and monopoly in the coffin furniture industry, 1870–1915', *EcHR*, 2nd ser., **19** (Dec. 1966), 621–41.

1414 Clapham, John H. 'The last years of the Navigation Acts', in *Ess. Ec. Hist.*, III, 144–78. Originally published 1910.

1415 Clements, Roger V. 'British trade unions and popular political economy, 1850–1875', *EcHR*, 2nd ser., **14** (Aug. 1961), 93–104.

1416 Cole, George D. H. 'Some notes on British trade unionism in the third quarter of the nineteenth century', in *Ess. Ec. Hist.*, III, 202–20. Originally published 1937.

1417 Cooney, E. W. 'Long waves in building in the British economy of the nineteenth century', *EcHR*, 2nd ser., **13** (Dec. 1960), 257–69.

1418 —— 'The origins of the Victorian master builders', *EcHR*, 2nd ser., **8** (Dec. 1955), 167–76.

1419 Coppock, Dennis J. 'British industrial growth during the "great depression" (1873–96): a pessimist's view', *EcHR*, 2nd ser., **17** (Dec. 1964), 389–96.

1420 —— 'The causes of the great depression, 1873–96', *Manchester School of Economic and Social Studies*, **29** (Sept. 1961), 205–32.

1421 —— 'The climacteric of the 1890's: a critical note', *Manchester School of Economic and Social Studies*, **24** (Jan. 1956), 1–31. A reply to (1468).

1422 Crouch, R. L. 'Laissez-faire in nineteenth century Britain: myth or reality?' *Manchester School of Economic and Social Studies*, **35** (Sept. 1967), 199–215.

1423 Davis, Lance E. and Jonathan R. T. Hughes. 'A dollar–sterling exchange, 1803–1895', *EcHR*, 2nd ser., **13** (Aug. 1960), 52–78.

1424 Deane, Phyllis. 'Contemporary estimates of the national income in the first half of the nineteenth century', *EcHR*, 2nd ser., **8** (Apr. 1956), 339–54.

1425 —— 'Contemporary estimates of national income in the second half of the nineteenth century', *EcHR*, 2nd ser., **9** (Apr. 1957), 451–61.

1426 Douglas, Paul H. 'An estimate of the growth of capital in the U.K., 1865–1909', *Journal of Economic and Business History*, **2** (Aug. 1930), 659–84.

1427 Duffy, Albert E. P. 'New unionism in Britain, 1889–1890, a reappraisal', *EcHR*, 2nd ser., **14** (Dec. 1961), 306–19.

1428 Fairlie, S. 'The nineteenth-century Corn Law reconsidered', *EcHR*, 2nd ser., **18** (Dec. 1965), 562–75.

1429 Falkus, M. E. 'The British gas industry before 1850', *EcHR*, 2nd ser., **20** (Dec. 1967), 494–508.

1430 Feinstein, Charles H. 'Income and investment in the United Kingdom, 1856–1914', *Economic Journal*, **71** (June, Dec. 1961), 367–85, 856–9.

1431 Fishlow, Albert. 'The trustee savings banks, 1817–1861', *JEcH*, **21** (Mar. 1961), 26–40.

1432 Ford, Alec G. 'Notes on the role of exports in British economic fluctuations, 1870–1914', *EcHR*, 2nd ser., **16** (Dec. 1963), 328–50.
1433 Foulke, Robert D. 'Life in the dying world of sail', *JBS*, **3** (Nov. 1963), 105–36.
1434 Fox, Alan. 'Industrial relations in nineteenth-century Birmingham', *Oxford Economic Papers*, **7** (Feb. 1955), 57–70.
1435 Graham, Gerald S. 'The ascendancy of the sailing ship 1850–85', *EcHR*, **9** (Aug. 1956), 74–88.
1436 —— 'Imperial finance, trade, and communications, 1895–1914', in *CHBE*, III, 438–89.
1437 Gupta, P. S. 'Railway trade unionism in Britain, *c.* 1880–1900', *EcHR*, 2nd ser., **19** (Apr. 1966), 124–53.
1438 Habakkuk, Hrothgar J. 'The economic history of modern Britain', *JEcH*, **18** (Dec. 1958), 486–501. A study of the relationship between population pressures and economic history.
1439 —— 'Fluctuations in house-building in Britain and the United States in the nineteenth century', *JEcH*, **22** (June 1962), 198–230.
1440 —— 'Free trade and commercial expansion, 1853–1870', in *CHBE*, II, 751–805.
1441 Harrison, Royden. 'British labor and American slavery', *Science and Society*, **25** (Dec. 1961), 291–319. The effect of the Civil War upon the British labour movement.
1442 Hartwell, Ronald M. 'The rising standard of living in England, 1800–1850', *EcHR*, 2nd ser., **13** (Apr. 1961), 397–416. Cf. (1443).
1443 Hobsbawm, Eric J. 'The British standard of living, 1790–1850', *EcHR*, 2nd ser., **10** (Aug. 1957), 46–61. Argues a decline in the working class's standard of living.
1444 —— 'Economic fluctuations and some social movements since 1800', *EcHR*, 2nd ser., **5** (no. 1, 1952), 1–25.
1445 —— 'General labour unions in Britain, 1889–1914', *EcHR*, 2nd ser., **1** (Aug. 1948), 123–42. On the continued distinction between skilled and unskilled workers.
1446 Hughes, Jonathan R. T. 'The commercial crisis of 1857', *Oxford Economic Papers*, **8** (June 1956), 194–222.
1447 Hughes, Jonathan R. T. and Stanley Reiter. 'The first 1,945 British steam-ships', *Journal of the American Statistical Association*, **53** (June 1958), 360–81.
1448 Hughes, Thomas P. 'British electrical industry lag: 1882–1888', *Technology and Culture*, **3** (Winter 1962), 27–44.
1449 Imlah, Albert H. 'Real values in British foreign trade, 1798–1853', *JEcH*, **8** (Nov. 1948), 133–52.
1450 Jefferys, James B. 'The denomination and character of shares, 1855–1885', in *Ess. Ec. Hist.*, I, 344–57.
1451 Kellett, J. R. 'Glasgow's railways, 1830–80: a study in natural growth', *EcHR*, 2nd ser., **17** (Dec. 1964), 354–68.
1452 Kenwood, A. G. 'Port investment in England and Wales, 1851–1913', *Yorkshire Bulletin of Economic and Social Research*, **17** (Nov. 1965), 156–67.
1453 —— 'Railway investment in Britain, 1825–1875', *Economica*, **32** (Aug. 1965), 313–22.
1454 Kindleberger, Charles P. 'Foreign trade and economic growth: lessons from Britain and France, 1850 to 1913', *EcHR*, 2nd ser., **14** (Dec. 1961), 289–305.
1455 Lenfant, J. H. 'Great Britain's capital formation, 1865–1914', *Economica*, **18** (May 1951), 151–67.
1456 Lipsey, Richard G. 'The relation between unemployment and the rate of change of money wage rates in the United Kingdom, 1862–1957: a further analysis', *Economica*, **27** (Feb. 1960), 1–31. See (1469).
1457 McCormick, Brian J. and James E. Williams. 'The miners and the eight-hour day, 1863–1910', *EcHR*, 2nd ser., **12** (Dec. 1959), 222–38.
1458 Maiwald, K. 'The construction costs and value of the British merchant

fleet, 1850–1938', *Scottish Journal of Political Economy*, **3** (Feb. 1956), 44–66.

1459 Maiwald, K. 'An index of building costs in the United Kingdom, 1845–1938', *EcHR*, 2nd ser., **7** (Dec. 1954), 187–203.

1460 Matthews, Robert C. O. 'The trade cycle in Britain, 1790–1850', *Oxford Economic Papers*, **6** (Feb. 1954), 1–32.

1461 Mitchell, Brian R. 'The coming of the railway and United Kingdom economic growth', *JEcH*, **24** (Sept. 1964), 315–36.

1462 Musson, Alfred E. 'The great depression in Britain, 1873–1896: a reappraisal', *JEcH*, **19** (June 1959), 199–228.

1463 North, Douglass C. 'Ocean freight rates and economic development, 1750–1913', *JEcH*, **18** (Dec. 1958), 537–55.

1464 O'Neill, Thomas P. 'From famine to near famine, 1845–1879', *Studia Hibernica*, **1** (1961), 161–71.

1465 Payne, Peter L. 'The emergence of the large-scale company in Great Britain, 1870–1914', *EcHR*, 2nd ser., **20** (Dec. 1967), 519–42.

1466 Pelling, Henry. 'The Knights of Labour in Britain, 1880–1901', *EcHR*, 2nd ser., **9** (Dec. 1956), 313–31.

1467 Phelps Brown, Ernest H. and Bernard Weber. 'Accumulation, productivity and distribution in the British economy, 1870–1938', in *Ess. Ec. Hist.*, III, 280–301.

1468 Phelps Brown, Ernest H. and Stephen J. Handfield-Jones. 'The climacteric of the 1890's: a study in the expanding economy', *Oxford Economic Papers*, **4** (Oct. 1952), 266–307. On the check to industrial production in the 1890s; see (1421).

1469 Phillips, A. W. 'The relation between unemployment and the rate of change of money wage rates in the United Kingdom, 1861–1957', *Economica*, **25** (Nov. 1958), 283–99. See the comment by Guy Routh, *ibid.*, **26** (Nov. 1959), 299–315. See also (1456).

1470 Platt, D. C. M. 'The role of the British consular service in overseas trade, 1825–1914', *EcHR*, 2nd ser., **15** (Apr. 1963), 494–512.

1471 Pollard, Sidney. 'Wages and earnings in the Sheffield trades, 1851–1914', *Yorkshire Bulletin of Economic and Social Research*, **6** (Feb. 1954), 49–64.

1472 Prest, Alan R. 'National income of the United Kingdom, 1870–1946', *Economic Journal*, **58** (Mar. 1948), 31–62.

1473 Richardson, H. W. 'Retardation in Britain's industrial growth, 1870–1913', *Scottish Journal of Political Economy*, **12** (June 1965), 125–49.

1474 Roberts, R. O. 'Bank of England branch discounting, 1826–59', *Economica*, **25** (Aug. 1958), 230–45.

1475 Sauerbeck, Augustus. 'Prices of commodities and the precious metals', in *Ess. Ec. Hist.*, III, 68–127.

1476 Saul, Samuel B. 'The export economy, 1870–1914', *Yorkshire Bulletin of Economic and Social Research*, **17** (May 1965), 5–18.

1477 —— 'House building in England 1890–1914', *EcHR*, 2nd ser., **15** (Aug. 1962), 119–37.

1478 —— 'The market and the development of the mechanical engineering industries in Britain, 1860–1914', *EcHR*, 2nd ser., **20** (Apr. 1967), 111–30.

1479 Saville, John. 'Sleeping partnerships and limited liability, 1850–1856', *EcHR*, 2nd ser., **8** (Apr. 1956), 418–33.

1480 Sayers, Richard S. 'Monetary thought and monetary policy in England', *Economic Journal*, **70** (Dec. 1960), 710–24.

1481 Segal, Harvey H. and Matthew Simon. 'British foreign capital issues, 1865–1894', *JEcH*, **21** (Dec. 1961), 566–81.

1482 Shannon, Herbert A. 'Bricks—a trade index, 1785–1849', in *Ess. Ec. Hist.*, III, 188–201.

1483 —— 'The coming of general limited liability', in *Ess. Ec. Hist.*, I, 358–79.

1484 —— 'The limited companies of 1866–1883', in *Ess. Ec. Hist.*, I, 380–405.

1485 Simon, Matthew. 'The enterprise and industrial composition of new British portfolio foreign investment, 1865–1914', *Journal of Development Studies*, **3** (Apr. 1967), 280–92.

1486 Singer, Hans W. 'An index of urban land rents and house rents in England and Wales, 1845–1913', *Econometrica*, 9 (July–Oct. 1941), 221–30.

1487 Spring, David. 'The Earls of Durham and the great northern coal field, 1830–1880', *Canadian Historical Review*, 33 (Sept. 1952), 237–53.

1488 Taylor, Arthur J. 'Concentration and specialization in the Lancashire cotton industry, 1825–1850', *EcHR*, 2nd ser., 1 (1949), 114–22.

1489 —— 'Labour productivity and technological innovation in the British coal industry, 1850–1914', *EcHR*, 2nd ser., 14 (Aug. 1961), 48–70.

1490 Thomas, Joan. 'A history of the Leeds clothing industry', *Yorkshire Bulletin of Economic and Social Research*, Occasional Papers no. 1 (Jan. 1955), 1–62.

1491 Thompson, Francis M. L. 'The land market in the nineteenth century', *Oxford Economic Papers*, 9 (Oct. 1957), 285–308.

1492 Tucker, Rufus S. 'Real wages of artisans in London, 1729–1935', *Journal of the American Statistical Association*, 31 (Mar. 1936), 73–84.

1493 Ward-Perkins, Charles N. 'The commercial crisis of 1847', in *Ess. Ec. Hist.*, III, 263–79.

1494 Williams, David M. 'Merchanting in the first half of the nineteenth century: the Liverpool timber trade', *Business History*, 8 (July 1966), 103–21.

1495 Williams, James E. 'The British standard of living, 1750–1850', *EcHR*, 2nd ser., 19 (Dec. 1966), 581–9.

1496 Williams, Lawrence J. 'The new unionism in south Wales, 1889–92', *Welsh History Review*, 1 (no. 4, 1963), 413–29.

1497 Williamson, Jeffrey G. 'The long swing: comparisons and interactions between British and American balance of payments, 1820–1913', *JEcH*, 22 (Mar. 1962), 21–46.

1498 Wilson, Charles. 'Economy and society in late Victorian Britain', *EcHR*, 2nd ser., 18 (Aug. 1965), 183–98. A revisionary analysis of the 'great depression'.

1499 Wood, George H. 'Real wages and the standard of comfort since 1850', in *Ess. Ec. Hist.*, III, 132–43.

IX AGRICULTURAL HISTORY

1 Printed sources

1500 Haggard, Henry Rider. *Rural England, being an account of agricultural and social researches carried out in the years 1901 and 1902 . . .* 1902, 2 vols.

1501 Hall, Alfred D. *The book of the Rothamsted experiments.* 1905. Includes a biographical introduction on Sir John Lawes and Sir Joseph Gilbert.

1502 Parker, John Oxley (ed.). *The Oxley Parker papers. From the letters and diaries of an Essex family of land agents in the nineteenth century.* Colchester, 1964.

2 Surveys

1503 Chambers, Jonathan D. and Gordon E. Mingay. *The agricultural revolution; 1750–1880.* 1966. A major revision of (1504).

1504 Ernle, Rowland E. Prothero, Baron. *English farming, past and present.* 6th ed., with introductions by George E. Fussell and Oliver R. McGregor. 1961. The standard survey, but the introductions are necessary to bring it up to date.

1505 Orwin, Charles S. *A history of English farming.* 1949.

1506 Orwin, Christabel S. and Edith H. Whetham. *History of British agriculture, 1846–1914.* 1964.

1507 Trow-Smith, Robert. *English husbandry, from the earliest times to the present day.* 1951.

3 Monographs
(See also sec. VII, pt. 3, above.)

1508 Bull, Leonard. *History of the Smithfield Club from 1798 to 1925.* 1926.
1509 Fussell, George E. *The English dairy farmer, 1500–1900.* 1966.
1510 —— *The farmer's tools, 1500–1900: the history of British farm implements, tools, and machinery before the tractor came.* 1952.
1511 —— *Farming systems from Elizabethan to Victorian days in the North and East Ridings of Yorkshire.* York, 1944.
1512 Grigg, David B. *The agricultural revolution in south Lincolnshire.* Cambridge, 1966. An important study, 1750–1850.
1513 Harris, Alan. *The rural landscape of the East Riding of Yorkshire, 1700–1850; a study in historical geography.* 1961.
1514 Hooker, Elizabeth R. *Readjustments of agricultural tenure in Ireland.* Chapel Hill, 1938.
1515 Hoskins, William G. *The making of the English landscape.* 1955.
1516 Hoskins, William G. and L. Dudley Stamp. *The common lands of England and Wales.* 1963. A brief historical survey and a full geographical survey of surviving common lands.
1517 Houston, George. *A history of the Scottish farm workers, 1800–1850.* Wakefield, 1964.
1518 Russell, E. John. *A history of agricultural science in Great Britain, 1620–1954.* 1966.
1519 Russell, Rex C. *The 'revolt of the field' in Lincolnshire.* Louth, 1956. On the unionization of agricultural labourers.
1520 Seebohm, Mabel E. *The evolution of the English farm.* 2nd ed., 1952.
1521 Spence, Clark C. *God speed the plow: the coming of steam cultivation to Great Britain.* Urbana, 1960.
1522 Spring, David. *The English landed estate in the nineteenth century: its administration.* Baltimore, 1963. Emphasizes primarily the Duke of Bedford's estates.
1523 Thirsk, Joan. *English peasant farming: the agrarian history of Lincolnshire from Tudor to recent times.* 1957.
1524 —— *Suffolk farming in the nineteenth century.* Ipswich, 1958.
1525 Trow-Smith, Robert. *A history of British livestock husbandry, 1700–1900.* 1959.
1526 Watson, James A. Scott. *The history of the Royal Agricultural Society of England, 1839–1939.* 1939.

4 Biographies

1527 Ashby, Mabel K. *Joseph Ashby of Tysoe, 1859–1919: a study of English village life.* Cambridge, 1961. An excellent biography of a farm labourer.

5 Articles

1528 Armytage, Walter H. G. 'The chartist land colonies 1846–1848', *Agricultural History*, **32** (Apr. 1958), 87–96.
1529 Beastall, T. W. 'A South Yorkshire estate in the late nineteenth century', *AgHR*, **14** (pt. I, 1966), 40–44.
1530 Collins, E. J. T. and Eric L. Jones. 'Sectoral advance in English agriculture, 1850–80', *AgHR*, **15** (pt. II, 1967), 65–81.
1531 Coppock, John T. 'Agricultural changes in the Chilterns, 1875–1900', *AgHR*, **9** (pt. I, 1961), 1–16.
1532 —— 'The statistical assessment of British agriculture', *AgHR*, **4** (pts. I–II, 1956), 4–21, 66–79.
1533 Drescher, Leo. 'The development of agricultural production in Great Britain and Ireland from the early nineteenth century', *The Manchester School of Economic and Social Studies*, **23** (May 1955), 153–83.

1534 Dunbabin, John P. D. 'The "revolt of the field": the agricultural labourers' movement in the 1870s', *PP*, no. 26 (Nov. 1963), 68–97.

1535 Erickson, Arvel B. 'The cattle plague in England, 1865–1867', *Agricultural History*, **35** (Apr. 1961), 94–103.

1536 Fletcher, T. W. 'The great depression of English agriculture, 1873–1896', *EcHR*, 2nd ser., **13** (Apr. 1961), 417–32.

1537 —— 'Lancashire livestock farming during the great depression', *AgHR*, **9** (pt. I, 1961), 17–42.

1538 Fussell, George E. 'The dawn of high farming in England: land reclamation in early Victorian days', *Agricultural History*, **22** (Apr. 1948), 83–95.

1539 —— 'English agriculture from Cobbett to Caird (1830–80)', *EcHR*, **15** (nos. 1–2, 1945), 79–85.

1540 Hall, Sherwin A. 'The cattle plague of 1865', *Medical History*, **6** (Jan. 1962), 45–58.

1541 Hunt, Edward H. 'Labour productivity in English agriculture, 1850–1914', *EcHR*, 2nd ser., **20** (Aug. 1967), 280–92.

1542 Jones, E. L. 'The changing basis of English agricultural prosperity, 1853–73', *AgHR*, **10** (pt. II, 1962), 102–19.

1543 —— 'English farming before and during the nineteenth century', *EcHR*, 2nd ser., **15** (Aug. 1962), 145–52.

1544 —— 'The agricultural labour market in England, 1793–1872', *EcHR*, 2nd ser., **17** (Dec. 1964), 322–38.

1545 Long, W. Harwood. 'The development of mechanisation in English farming', *AgHR*, **11** (pt. I, 1963), 15–26.

1546 Moore, D. Cresap. 'The corn laws and high farming', *EcHR*, 2nd ser., **18** (Dec. 1965), 546–68.

1547 Olson, Mancur L., Jr. and Curtis C. Harris, Jr. 'Free trade in "corn": a statistical study of the prices and production of wheat in Great Britain from 1873 to 1914', *Quarterly Journal of Economics*, **73** (Feb. 1959), 145–68.

1548 Robinson, O. 'The London companies as progressive landlords in nineteenth century Ireland', *EcHR*, 2nd ser., **15** (Aug. 1962), 103–18.

1549 Shearman, Hugh. 'State aided land purchase under the disestablishment act of 1869', *IHS*, **4** (Mar. 1944), 58–80.

1550 Sheppard, June A. 'East Yorkshire's agricultural labour force in the mid-nineteenth century', *AgHR*, **9** (pt. I, 1961), 43–54.

1551 Spring, David. 'The English landed estate in the age of coal and iron: 1830–1880', *JEcH*, **2** (Winter 1951), 3–24.

1552 Sturgess, R. W. 'The agricultural revolution in the English clays', *AgHR*, **14** (pt. II, 1966), 104–21, **15** (pt. II, 1967), 82–7.

1553 Thompson, Francis M. L. 'English great estates in the 19th century, 1790–1914', in *First International Conference of Economic History*. Stockholm, 1960, pp. 385–97.

1554 —— 'The second agricultural revolution, 1815–1880', *EcHR*, 2nd ser., **21** (Apr. 1968), 62–77.

1555 Thompson, Robert J. 'An inquiry into the rent of agricultural land in England and Wales during the nineteenth century', *Journal of the Royal Statistical Society*, **70** (Dec. 1907), 587–616.

1556 Ward, John T. 'The Beaumont family's estates in the nineteenth century', *BIHR*, **35** (Nov. 1962), 169–77.

1557 Wheeler, Philip T. 'Landownership and the crofting system in Sutherland since 1800', *AgHR*, **14** (pt. I, 1966), 45–56.

1558 Whetham, Edith H. 'Livestock prices in Britain, 1851–93', *AgHR*, **11** (pt. I, 1963), 27–35.

1559 —— 'The London milk trade, 1860–1900', *EcHR*, 2nd ser., **17** (Dec. 1964), 369–80.

1560 —— 'Prices and production in Scottish farming, 1850–1870', *Scottish Journal of Political Economy*, **9** (Nov. 1962), 233–43.

X SCIENCE AND TECHNOLOGY

1 Printed sources

1561 Barlow, Nora (ed.). *Darwin and Henslow: the growth of an idea; letters 1831–1860.* 1967.
1562 Darwin, Charles. *The autobiography of Charles Darwin 1809–1882 with original omissions restored,* ed. Nora Barlow. 1958.
1563 —— *The origin of species: a variorum text,* ed. Morse Peckham. Philadelphia, 1959. See also the facsimile of the first edition (1859) with an introduction by Ernst Mayr. 1964.
1564 De Beer, Gavin (ed.). *Charles Darwin and Alfred Russel Wallace, evolution by natural selection.* Cambridge, 1958.
1565 —— 'Further unpublished letters of Charles Darwin', *Annals of Science,* 14 (June 1958), 83–115.
1566 Jones, Howard Mumford and I. Bernard Cohen, with the assistance of Everett Mendelsohn (eds.). *Science before Darwin: a nineteenth-century anthology.* 1963.
1567 *Medical register 1858–.* 1859–.
1568 *Reports of the meetings of the British Association for the Advancement of Science.* 1833–1938.
1569 Royal Society of London. *Proceedings.* 1832–1905, 75 vols.
1570 Wallace, Alfred Russel. *My life: a record of events and opinions.* 2nd ed., 1908.

2 Surveys

1571 Bernal, John D. *Science and industry in the nineteenth century.* 1953.
1572 Dampier [-Whetham], William C. *A history of science and its relations with philosophy and religion.* 4th ed., Cambridge, 1948. Reprinted with post-script by I. Bernard Cohen, Cambridge, 1961.
1573 Derry, Thomas K. and Trevor I. Williams. *A short history of technology from the earliest times to A.D. 1900.* Oxford, 1961.
1574 Dingle, Herbert (ed.). *A century of science, 1851–1951.* 1951.
1575 Singer, Charles J. *A short history of biology: a general introduction to the study of living things.* Oxford, 1931.
1576 —— *A short history of science in the nineteenth century.* 1941.
1577 Singer, Charles J. et al. *A history of technology,* IV, *The industrial revolution,* V, *The late nineteenth century.* Oxford, 1958.
1578 Singer, Charles J. and E. Ashworth Underwood. *A short history of medicine.* 2nd ed., Oxford, 1962.
1579 Taton, René (ed.). *General History of the sciences,* III, *Science in the nineteenth century,* trans. Arnold J. Pomerans. 1965.
1580 Taylor, Frank Sherwood. *The century of science.* 3rd ed., 1952.

3 Monographs

1581 Andrade, E. N. da Costa. *Rutherford and the nature of the atom.* Garden City, N.Y., 1964.
1582 Barnaby, Kenneth Cloves. *The Institution of Naval Architects, 1860–1960.* 1960.
1583 Bell, Peter R. (ed.). *Darwin's biological work: some aspects reconsidered.* 1959.
1584 Brock, William H. (ed.). *The atomic debates: Brodie and the rejection of the atomic theory; three studies.* Leicester, 1967. Controversies of the 1860s.
1585 Cardwell, Donald S. L. *The organisation of science in England: a retrospect.* 1957.
1586 Carter, George S. *A hundred years of evolution.* 1957.
1587 Clark, George. *A history of the Royal College of Physicians of London.* 2 vols., 1964–6.

1588 Clow, Archibald and Nan L. *The chemical revolution: a contribution to social technology.* 1952.
1589 Cope, Zachary. *Florence Nightingale and the doctors.* 1958.
1590 —— *The Royal College of Surgeons of England.* 1960.
1591 Domb, Cyril (ed.). *Clerk Maxwell and modern science: six commemorative lectures by Edward V. Appleton and others.* 1963.
1592 Eiseley, Loren C. *Darwin's century: evolution and the men who discovered it.* 1959.
1593 Gillispie, Charles C. *Genesis and geology, a study in the relations of scientific thought, natural theology, and social opinion in Great Britain, 1790–1850.* 1951.
1594 Glass, Bentley, Owsei Temkin and William L. Straus (eds.). *Forerunners of Darwin, 1745–1859.* Baltimore, 1959.
1595 Greenwood, Major. *Some British pioneers of social medicine.* 1948.
1596 Habakkuk, Hrothgar J. *American and British technology in the nineteenth century: the search for labour-saving inventions.* Cambridge, 1962. Factors in the relative decline of British entrepreneurship.
1597 Haber, Francis C. *The age of the world: Moses to Darwin.* Baltimore, 1959.
1598 Haines, George, IV. *German influence upon English education and science 1800–1866.* New London, Conn., 1957.
1599 Hammond, Rolt. *The Forth Bridge and its builders.* 1964.
1600 Hearnshaw, Leslie S. *A short history of British psychology, 1840–1940.* New York, 1964.
1601 Himmelfarb, Gertrude. *Darwin and the Darwinian revolution.* New York, 1959. A controversial treatment of Darwin's work.
1602 Hogben, Lancelot. *Science for the citizen; a self-educator based on the social background of scientific discovery.* 1938.
1603 Hooykaas, Reijer. *Natural law and divine miracle; a historical-critical study of the principle of uniformity in geology, biology and theology.* Leiden, 1959.
1604 Howarth, Osbert J. R. *The British Association for the Advancement of Science: a retrospect 1831–1921.* 2nd ed., 1931.
1605 Ihde, Aaron J. *The development of modern chemistry.* New York, 1964. A very detailed study.
1606 Irvine, William. *Apes, angels, and Victorians: the story of Darwin, Huxley, and evolution.* New York, 1955.
1607 Larsen, Egon. *The Cavendish Laboratory.* 1962.
1608 Leigh, Denis. *The historical development of British psychiatry,* I. Oxford, 1961.
1609 Lloyd, Christopher and Jack L. S. Coulter. *Medicine and the Navy, 1200–1900,* IV, *1815–1900.* Edinburgh, 1963.
1610 Loewenberg, Bert J. *Darwin, Wallace, and the theory of natural selection: including the Linnean Society papers.* Cambridge, Mass., 1959.
1611 MacDonald, David K. C. *Faraday, Maxwell, and Kelvin.* Garden City, N.Y., 1964.
1612 Matthews, Leslie G. *History of pharmacy in Britain.* Edinburgh, 1962.
1613 Millhauser, Milton. *Just before Darwin: Robert Chambers and "Vestiges".* Middletown, Conn., 1959.
1614 Newman, Charles. *The evolution of medical education in the nineteenth century.* 1957.
1615 Partington, James R. *A history of chemistry,* IV. 1964.
1616 Sears, Paul B. *Charles Darwin, the naturalist as a cultural force.* New York, 1950.
1617 Sharlin, Harold I. *The convergent century: the unification of science in the nineteenth century.* New York, 1966.
1618 Sykes, W. Stanley. *Essays on the first hundred years of anaesthesia.* Edinburgh, 1960–1, 2 vols.
1619 Wiener, Philip and Aaron Noland (eds.). *Roots of scientific thought.* New York, 1957. Articles on evolution.
1620 Willey, Basil. *Darwin and Butler: two versions of evolution.* 1960.

3-2

4 Biographies

1621   Allan, Mea. *The Hookers of Kew, 1785–1911.* 1967.
1622   Bailey, Edward. *Charles Lyell.* 1962.
1623   Bibby, H. Cyril. *T. H. Huxley: scientist, humanist, and educator.* 1959.
1624   Brook, Charles W. *Battling surgeon.* Glasgow, 1945. A life of Thomas Wakley, founder of the *Lancet.*
1625   Burnie, Robert W. *Memoir and letters of Sidney Gilchrist Thomas, inventor.* 1891.
1626   Cameron, Hector C. *Joseph Lister: the friend of man.* 1948. Somewhat popular.
1627   Cheyne, William W. *Lister and his achievement.* 1925.
1628   Cohen, John M. *The life of Ludwig Mond.* 1956.
1629   Cope, Zachary. *Sir John Tomes: a pioneer of British dentistry.* 1961.
1630   Crowther, James G. *British scientists of the nineteenth century.* 1935. Davy, Faraday, Joule, Thomson and Clerk Maxwell.
1631   —— *Statesmen of science: Henry Brougham, William Robert Grove, Lyon Playfair, the Prince Consort, the seventh Duke of Devonshire, Alexander Strange, Richard ⟨Burdon Haldane, Henry Thomas Tizard and Frederick Alexander Lindemann.* 1965.
1632   Darwin, Francis. *The life and letters of Charles Darwin.* 3 vols., 1887. Reprinted, 2 vols., New York, 1959.
1633   De Beer, Gavin R. *Charles Darwin: evolution by natural selection.* 1963.
1634   Eyre, John V. *Henry Edward Armstrong, 1848–1937: the doyen of British chemists and pioneer of technical education.* 1958.
1635   George, Wilma. *Biologist philosopher: a study of the life and writings of Alfred Russel Wallace.* 1964.
1636   Gibbs-Smith, Charles H. *Sir George Cayley's aeronautics, 1796–1855.* 1962. See also (1646).
1637   Godlee, Rickman. *Lord Lister.* 1917.
1638   Huxley, Julian S. and Henry B. D. Kettlewell. *Charles Darwin and his world.* 1965.
1639   Huxley, Leonard. *Life and letters of Sir Joseph Dalton Hooker.* 2 vols., 1918.
1640   —— *Life and letters of Thomas Huxley.* 3 vols., 1903.
1641   Lyell, Katharine M. (ed.). *Life, letters, and journals of Sir Charles Lyell, Bart.* 2 vols., 1881.
1642   McMenemy, William H. *The life and times of Sir Charles Hastings, founder of the British Medical Association.* Edinburgh, 1959.
1643   Manson-Bahr, Philip. *Patrick Manson, the father of tropical medicine.* 1962.
1644   Marchant, James. *Alfred Russel Wallace: letters and reminiscences.* 2 vols., 1916.
1645   Moseley, Maboth. *Irascible genius: a life of Charles Babbage, inventor.* 1964.
1646   Pritchard, John L. *Sir George Cayley, the inventor of the aeroplane.* 1961.
1647   Rayleigh, Robert J. Strutt, 4th Baron. *Life of John William Strutt, third Baron Rayleigh, O.M., F.R.S.* Augmented ed., Madison, Wis., 1968.
1648   Reid, Thomas Wemyss. *Memoirs and correspondence of Lyon Playfair, first Lord Playfair of St. Andrews, P.C., G.C.B., Ll.D., F.R.S., &c.* 1899.
1649   Rolt, Lionel T. C. *George and Robert Stephenson; the railway revolution.* 1960.
1650   —— *Isambard Kingdom Brunel: a biography.* 1957.
1651   Shepherd, John A. *Spencer Wells: the life and work of a Victorian surgeon.* Edinburgh, 1965.
1652   Thompson, Lillian G. *Sidney Gilchrist Thomas.* 1940.
1653   Thomson, George. *J. J. Thomson and the Cavendish Laboratory in his day.* 1964.
1654   Todhunter, Isaac. *William Whewell.* 2 vols., 1876.
1655   Turrill, William B. *Joseph Dalton Hooker, botanist, explorer, and administrator.* 1963.
1656   West, Geoffrey [pseud. of Geoffrey H. Wells]. *Charles Darwin, the fragmentary man.* 1937.

1657   Wichler, Gerhard. *Charles Darwin: the founder of the theory of evolution and natural selection.* Oxford, 1961.

1658   Williams, L. Pearce. *Michael Faraday, a biography.* New York. 1965.

1659   Williams-Ellis, Amabel. *Darwin's moon: a biography of Alfred Russel Wallace.* 1966.

5 Articles

(See also sec. XIV, pt. 5, below.)

1660   Bernstein, Henry T. 'J. Clerk Maxwell on the history of the kinetic theory of gases, 1871', *Isis*, **54** (June 1963), 206–16.

1661   Bibby, Cyril. 'Huxley and the reception of the "Origin"', *VS*, **3** (Sept. 1959), 76–86.

1662   Cannon, Walter F. 'The bases of Darwin's achievement: a revaluation', *VS*, **5** (Dec. 1961), 109–34.

1663   —— 'History in depth: the early Victorian period', in Crombie, Alistair C. and Michael A. Hoskin (eds.). *History of science: an annual review of literature, research, and teaching*, III. Cambridge, 1964, pp. 20–38.

1664   —— 'The normative role of science in early Victorian thought', *JHI*, **25** (Oct. 1964), 487–502.

1665   —— 'The problem of miracles in the 1830's', *VS*, **4** (Sept. 1960), 5–32.

1666   —— 'Scientists and broad churchmen: an early Victorian intellectual network', *JBS*, **4** (Nov. 1964), 65–88. Important for the social history of the intellectual élite.

1667   —— 'The uniformitarian–catastrophist debate,' *Isis*, **51** (Mar. 1960), 38–55. A provocative revision.

1668   Crellin, J. K. 'Pharmaceutical history and its sources in the Wellcome collections. I. The growth of professionalism in nineteenth-century British pharmacy', *Medical History*, **11** (July 1967), 215–27.

1669   De Beer, Gavin. 'Charles Darwin', *Proceedings of the British Academy*, **44** (1959), 163–83.

1670   Ducasse, Curt J. 'Whewell's philosophy of scientific discovery', *Philosophical Review*, **60** (Jan. 1951), 59–69 (Apr. 1951), 213–34.

1671   Eiseley, Loren C. 'Charles Darwin, Edward Blyth, and the theory of natural selection', *Proceedings of the American Philosophical Society*, **103** (1959), 94–158. Argues that Darwin unconsciously borrowed from Blyth.

1672   —— 'Darwin, Coleridge and the theory of unconscious creation', *Daedalus*, **94** (Summer 1965), 588–602.

1673   Evans, Mary Alice. 'Mimicry and the Darwinian heritage', *JHI*, **26** (Apr. 1965), 211–20. The progress of research on protective adaptation.

1674   Fleck, George M. 'Atomism in late nineteenth-century physical chemistry', *JHI*, **24** (Jan. 1963), 106–14.

1675   Forbes, Thomas R. 'William Yarrell, British naturalist', *Proceedings of the American Philosophical Society*, **106** (1962), 505–15.

1676   Greenaway, Frank. 'A Victorian scientist: the experiment researches of Sir William Crookes (1832–1919)', *Proceedings of the Royal Institution of Great Britain*, **39** (pt. 2, 1962), 172–98.

1677   Haines, George, IV. 'German influence upon scientific instruction in England, 1867–1887', *VS*, **1** (Mar. 1958), 215–44.

1678   Hopley, I. B. 'Clerk Maxwell's apparatus for the measurement of surface tension', *Annals of Science*, **13** (Sept. 1957), 180–7.

1679   —— 'Maxwell's determination of the number of electrostatic units in one electromagnetic unit of electricity', *Annals of Science*, **15** (June 1959), 91–108.

1680   —— 'Maxwell's work on electrical resistance', *Annals of Science*, **13** (Dec. 1957), 265–72, **14** (Sept. 1958), 197–210, **15** (Mar. 1959), 51–5.

1681   Hooykaas, Reijer. 'The principle of uniformity in geology, biology, and theology', *Journal of the Transactions of the Victoria Institute*, **88** (1956), 101–16.

1682   Huxley, Francis. 'Charles Darwin: life and habit', *American Scholar*, **28** (Fall 1959), 489–99, **29** (Winter 1959–60), 85–93.

1683 Huxley, Julian. 'The emergence of Darwinism', in Tax, Sol (ed.). *Evolution after Darwin*, I, *Evolution of life*. Chicago, 1960, pp. 1–22.

1684 Kelham, Brian B. 'The Royal College of Science for Ireland (1867–1926)', *Studies*, **56** (Autumn 1967), 297–309.

1685 Loewenberg, Bert J. 'The mosaic of Darwinian thought', *VS*, **3** (Sept. 1959), 3–18.

1686 McKinney, H. Lewis. 'Alfred Russel Wallace and the discovery of natural selection', *Journal of the History of Medicine*, **21** (Oct. 1966), 333–57.

1687 MacLeod, Roy M. 'Evolutionism and Richard Owen, 1830–1868: an episode in Darwin's century', *Isis*, **56** (Fall 1965), 259–80.

1688 Magoun, Horace W. 'Evolutionary concepts of brain function following Darwin and Spencer', in Tax, Sol (ed.). *Evolution after Darwin*, II, *Evolution of man*. Chicago, 1960, pp. 187–209.

1689 Mendelsohn, Everett. 'The biological sciences in the nineteenth century: some problems and sources', in Crombie, Alistair C. and Michael A. Hoskin (eds.). *History of science: an annual review of literature, research, and teaching*, III. Cambridge, 1964, pp. 39–59.

1690 Paden, William D. 'Arthur O'Shaughnessy in the British Museum; or, the case of the misplaced fusees and the reluctant zoologist', *VS*, **8** (Sept. 1964), 7–30. The poet as zoologist: a glimpse into the politics of the British Museum.

1691 Scott, Wilson L. 'The significance of "hard bodies" in the history of scientific thought', *Isis*, **50** (Sept. 1959), 199–210.

1692 Selwyn, S. 'Sir James Simpson and hospital cross-infection', *Medical History*, **9** (July 1965), 241–8.

1693 Strong, Edward W. 'William Whewell and John Stuart Mill: their controversy about scientific knowledge', *JHI*, **16** (Apr. 1955), 209–31.

1694 Thompson, Denys. 'John Tyndall and the Royal Institution', *Annals of Science*, **13** (Mar. 1957), 9–21.

1695 Vorzimmer, Peter. 'Charles Darwin and blending inheritance', *Isis*, **54** (Sept. 1963), 371–90.

1696 —— 'Darwin's ecology and its influence upon his theory', *Isis*, **56** (Summer 1965), 148–55.

1697 Webb, David A. 'William Henry Harvey, 1811–1866, and the tradition of systematic botany', *Hermathena*, **103** (Autumn 1966), 32–45.

1698 Willey, Basil. 'Darwin's place in the history of thought', in Banton, Michael P. (ed.). *Darwinism and the study of society, a centenary symposium*. London, 1961, pp. 1–16.

XI MILITARY AND NAVAL HISTORY

1 Printed sources

1699 Baylen, Joseph O. and Alan Conway (eds.). *Soldier-surgeon: the Crimean war letters of Dr. Douglas A. Reid, 1855–1856*. Knoxville, 1958.

1700 Bonner-Smith, David (ed.). *Russian war, 1855, Baltic; official correspondence* (Navy Records Society, LXXXIV). 1944.

1701 Bonner-Smith, David and Alfred C. Dewar (eds.). *Russian war, 1854, Baltic and Black Sea; official correspondence* (Navy Records Society, LXXXIII). 1943.

1702 Bonner-Smith, David and Esmond W. R. Lumby (eds.). *The second China war, 1856–1860* (Navy Records Society, XCV). 1954.

1703 *Brassey's annual: the armed forces year-book*. 1886–.

1704 Dewar, Alfred C. (ed.). *Russian war, 1855, Black Sea; official correspondence* (Navy Records Society, LXXXV). 1945.

1705 Hart, Henry G. (ed.). *The new army list*. 1839–1901. Annual; subtitle varies; includes militia after 1870.

1706   Russell, William H. *The British expedition to the Crimea*. Rev. ed., 1877.
Reports of *The Times*' correspondent.
1707   Thompson, Paul (ed.). *Close to the wind: the early (1866–1879) memoirs of
Admiral Sir William Cresswell*. 1965.
1708   Wolseley, Garnet J., 1st Viscount. *The story of a soldier's life*. 1903, 2 vols.

2   Surveys

1709   Clowes, William L. *et al. The royal navy: a history*, VI–VII. 1902–3.
1710   Fortescue, John W. *A history of the British army*, XI–XIII. 1923–30. The
standard history.
1711   Lewis, Michael. *The history of the British navy*. 1959.

3   Monographs

1712   Amery, Leopold S. *The Times history of the war in South Africa*. 1907, 6 vols.
1713   Bartlett, Christopher J. *Great Britain and sea power, 1815–1853*. Oxford,
1963.
1714   Baxter, James P., III. *The introduction of the ironclad warship*. Cambridge,
Mass., 1933.
1715   Biddulph, Sir Robert. *Lord Cardwell at the war office: a history of his
administration, 1868–1874*. 1904.
1716   Bond, Brian (ed.). *Victorian military campaigns: the Sikh wars; the third
China war, 1860; the expedition to Abyssinia, 1867–8; the Ashanti campaign,
1873–4; the South African war, 1880–1; the Egyptian campaign, 1882; the
reconquest of the Sudan*. 1967.
1717   Clarke, Ignatius F. *Voices prophesying war: 1763–1984*. 1966. Anticipations
of future wars, focusing on Chesney's *Battle of Dorking*.
1718   Cooper, Leonard. *British regular cavalry, 1644–1914*. 1966.
1719   DuCane, Hubert J. (tr.). *The war in South Africa, prepared by the historical
section of the Great General Staff, Berlin*. 1904–6, 2 vols.
1720   Ffoulkes, Charles J. and Edward C. Hopkinson. *Sword, lance and bayonet:
a record of the arms of the British army and navy*. Cambridge, 1938. 2nd
ed., New York, 1967.
1721   Gardner, Brian. *Mafeking: a Victorian legend*. 1966.
1722   Gibbs, Peter. *The battle of the Alma*. 1963.
1723   Graham, Gerald S. *The politics of naval supremacy: studies in British maritime
ascendancy*. 1965.
1724   Grant, Maurice H. *History of the war in South Africa*. 1910, 6 vols.
1725   Hamley, Edward B. *The war in the Crimea*. 1891.
1726   Hibbert, Christopher. *The destruction of Lord Raglan*. 1961.
1727   Holt, Edgar. *The Boer war*. 1958.
1728   Hough, Richard. *Admirals in collision*. 1959. The collision of the *Victoria*
and the *Camperdown*, 1893.
1729   Hurd, Douglas. *The Arrow war*. 1967.
1730   Johnson, Franklyn A. *Defence by committee: the British committee of imperial
defence 1885–1959*. 1960.
1731   Kinglake, Alexander W. *The invasion of the Crimea: its origin and an account
of its progress down to the death of Lord Raglan*. 6th ed., 1877–88, 9 vols.
A classic, though deficient on the non-military aspects.
1732   Kruger, Rayne. *Good-bye, Dolly Gray: the story of the Boer war*. Cambridge,
1959.
1733   Laffin, John. *Tommy Atkins: the story of the English soldier*. 1966.
1734   Lewis, Michael. *The navy in transition, 1814–1864*. 1965.
1735   Luvaas, Jay. *The education of an army: British military thought, 1815–1940*.
1965.
1736   Marder, Arthur J. *The anatomy of British sea power: a history of British naval
policy . . . 1880–1905*. New York, 1940.
1737   Maurice, John F. *History of the war in South Africa, 1899–1902*. 1906–10,
4 vols. and 4 portfolios of maps.

MILITARY AND NAVAL AFFAIRS

1738 Pemberton, W. Baring. *Battles of the Crimean war.* 1962.
1739 Preston, Antony and John Major. *Send a gunboat.* 1967. Naval and diplomatic history, 1854–1900.
1740 Roads, Christopher H. *The British soldier's firearm, 1850–1864.* 1964.
1741 Schurman, Donald M. *The education of a navy: the development of British naval strategic thought, 1867–1914.* Chicago, 1965.
1742 Symons, Julian. *Buller's campaign.* 1963.
1743 —— *England's pride: the story of the Gordon relief expedition.* 1965.
1744 Thomas, Hugh. *The story of Sandhurst.* 1961.
1745 Vulliamy, Colwyn E. *Crimea; the campaign of 1854–56 with an outline of politics and a study of the royal quartet.* 1939.
1746 Woodham-Smith, Cecil. *The reason why.* 1953. A scathing account of the British army during the Crimean war. See the critique in Brison D. Gooch. 'The Crimean war in selected documents and secondary works since 1940', *VS*, 1 (Mar. 1958), 271–9.

4 Biographies

1747 Arthur, George. *Life of Lord Kitchener.* 1920, 3 vols. The authorized biography.
1748 Churchill, Randolph S. *Winston S. Churchill,* I, *Youth 1874–1900.* 1966. By his son; of interest for more than military history.
1749 Elton, Godfrey. *General Gordon.* 1954.
1750 James, David. *Lord Roberts.* 1954.
1751 Lehmann, Joseph H. *All Sir Garnet; a life of Field-Marshal Lord Wolseley.* 1964. Published in America as *The model major-general.*
1752 Magnus, Philip. *Kitchener: portrait of an imperialist.* 1958.
1753 Maurice, Frederick B. and George Arthur. *The life of Lord Wolseley.* 1924.
1754 Napier, Henry D. *Field-Marshal Lord Napier of Magdala, G.C.B., G.C.S.I., a memoir.* 1927.
1755 Nutting, Anthony. *Gordon of Khartoum: martyr and misfit.* 1966.
1756 St Aubyn, Giles. *The royal George, 1819–1904: the life of H.R.H. Prince George, Duke of Cambridge.* 1963.
1757 Stuart, Vivian. *The beloved little admiral.* 1967. Henry Keppel, 1822–76.
1758 Williams, Hugh N. *The life and letters of Admiral Sir Charles Napier K.C.B.* 1917.

5 Articles

1759 Blanco, Richard L. 'Reform and Wellington's post-Waterloo army, 1815–1854', *Military Affairs,* 29 (Fall 1965), 123–31.
1760 Bond, Brian. 'Doctrine and training in the British cavalry, 1870–1914', in Michael Howard (ed.). *The theory and practice of war: essays presented to Captain B. H. Liddell Hart.* 1965, pp. 95–125.
1761 —— 'Recruiting the Victorian army', *VS*, 5 (June 1962), 331–8.
1762 Bourne, Kenneth. 'British preparations for war with the North', *EHR*, 76 (Oct. 1961), 600–32.
1763 Tucker, Albert V. 'Army and society in England 1870–1900: a reassessment of the Cardwell reforms', *JBS*, 2 (May 1963), 110–41.
1764 Tunstall, William C. B. 'Imperial defence, 1815–1870', in *CHBE*, II, 806–41.
1765 —— 'Imperial defence, 1870–1897', in *CHBE*, III, 230–54.

XII RELIGIOUS HISTORY

1 Printed sources

1766 Baker, E. P. (ed.). *Bishop Wilberforce's visitation returns for the archdeaconry of Oxford in the year 1854* (Oxfordshire Record Series, xxxv). Oxford, 1954.

1767 Blehl, Vincent F. 'Newman's delation: some hitherto unpublished letters', *Dublin Review*, **234** (Winter 1960–1), 296–305.

1768 *Census of Great Britain, 1851. Religious worship England and Wales* (Parliamentary Papers, House of Commons, 1852–3, LXXXIX). 1852. Highly flawed, this is none the less the only census of its kind and is an invaluable source for statistics of religious attendance.

1769 Chadwick, Owen (ed.). *The mind of the Oxford movement.* 1960.

1770 Cockshut, Anthony O. J. *Religious controversies of the nineteenth century: selected documents.* 1966.

1771 Conzemius, Victor (ed.). *Ignaz von Döllinger Briefwechsel mit Lord Acton.* München, 1963–5, 2 vols. A third volume (from 1870) will complete this superbly edited correspondence.

1772 *Correspondence of John Henry Newman with John Keble and others, 1839–1845.* 1917.

1773 *Crockford's clerical directory: a reference book of the clergy of the established Church of England and of the other churches in communion with the see of Canterbury.* 1858–. Annual, later biennial.

1774 Dessain, Charles Stephen (ed.). *Letters and diaries of John Henry Newman.* XI–. 1961–. Vol. XI begins with Oct. 1845. A major editorial enterprise.

1775 Fairweather, Eugene R. (ed.). *The Oxford movement.* New York, 1964.

1776 Figgis, John N. and Reginald V. Laurence (eds.). *Selections from the correspondence of the first Lord Acton.* 1917.

1777 Lathbury, Daniel C. (ed.). *Correspondence on church and religion of William Ewart Gladstone.* 1910, 2 vols.

1778 Mozley, Anne (ed.). *Letters and correspondence of John Henry Newman during his life in the English Church.* 1891, 2 vols.

1779 Newman, John H. *Apologia pro vita sua. The two versions of 1864 and 1865; preceded by Newman's and Kingsley's pamphlets,* ed. Wilfrid Ward. 1913.

1780 Paul, Herbert (ed.). *Letters of Lord Acton to Mary, daughter of the Right Hon. W. E. Gladstone.* 2nd ed., 1913.

1781 Spurgeon, Charles H. *C. H. Spurgeon's autobiography,* ed. Susannah Spurgeon and W. J. Harrald, 1899–1900, 4 vols.

2 Surveys

1782 Carpenter, Spencer C. *Church and people 1789–1889; a history of the Church of England from William Wilberforce to 'Lux Mundi'.* 1933.

1783 Chadwick, Owen. *The Victorian church,* I. 1966. Covers the period to 1860. The best general study.

1784 Elliott-Binns, Leonard E. *Religion in the Victorian era.* 2nd ed., 1964.

1785 Latourette, Kenneth S. *Christianity in a revolutionary age,* II, *The nineteenth century in Europe: the Protestant and eastern churches.* New York, 1959. Detailed, ecumenical, but not profound.

1786 Moorman, John R. H. *A history of the Church in England.* 1953.

1787 Vidler, Alec R. *The Church in an age of revolution: 1789 to the present day.* 1962. Insightful vignettes.

1788 Warre-Cornish, Francis. *The English Church in the nineteenth century* (History of the English Church, VIII–IX). 1910, 2 vols.

3 Monographs

1789 Addison, William G. *Religious equality in modern England 1714–1914.* 1944.
1790 Allchin, Arthur M. *The silent rebellion, Anglican religious communities 1845–1900.* 1958.
1791 Altholz, Josef L. *The liberal Catholic movement in England: the 'Rambler' and its contributors 1848–1864.* 1962.
1792 Anson, Peter F. *The call of the cloister; religious communities and kindred bodies in the Anglican communion,* ed. A. W. Campbell. 2nd ed., 1964.
1793 Arnold, Ralph. *The Whiston matter; the Reverend Robert Whiston versus the dean and chapter of Rochester.* 1961. A conflict over church charities fictionalized by Trollope in *The Warden.*
1794 Balleine, George R. *A history of the evangelical party in the Church of England.* New ed., 1951.
1795 Beck, George A. (ed.). *The English Catholics 1850–1950; essays to commemorate the centenary of the restoration of the hierarchy of England and Wales.* 1950. Includes some valuable contributions.
1796 Best, Geoffrey F. A. *Bishop Westcott and the miners.* Cambridge, 1967.
1797 —— *Temporal pillars: Queen Anne's Bounty, the Ecclesiastical Commissioners and the Church of England.* Cambridge, 1964. An excellent work on church finances.
1798 Binyon, G. Clive. *The Christian socialist movement in England: an introduction to the study of its history.* 1931.
1799 Blehl, Vincent F. and Francis X. Connolly (eds.). *Newman's Apologia: a classic reconsidered.* New York, 1964.
1800 Brilioth, Yngve. *The Anglican revival: studies in the Oxford movement.* 1925. An important contribution by a Swedish scholar.
1801 Brockett, Allan. *Nonconformity in Exeter, 1650–1875.* Manchester, 1962.
1802 Brose, Olive J. *Church and parliament: the reshaping of the Church of England, 1828–1860.* 1959.
1803 Brown, Charles K. F. *A history of the English clergy, 1800–1900.* 1953.
1804 Buchanan, Robert. *The ten years conflict: being the history of the disruption of the Church of Scotland.* Glasgow, 1849, 2 vols.
1805 Burleigh, John H. S. *Church history of Scotland.* 1960.
1806 Cameron, James M. *The night battle.* 1962. Includes an essay on Newman and empiricism.
1807 *Catholic emancipation 1829 to 1929. Essays by various writers.* 1929.
1808 Chadwick, Owen. *The founding of Cuddesdon.* Oxford, 1954.
1809 —— *From Bossuet to Newman: the idea of doctrinal development.* Cambridge, 1957. A delightful essay in intellectual history.
1810 Christensen, Torben. *Origin and history of Christian socialism, 1848–54* (Acta Theologica Danica, III). Aarhus, 1962. The most significant work on the subject.
1811 Church, Richard W. *The Oxford movement: twelve years, 1833–1845.* Rev. ed., 1891. The classic sympathetic account, still worth reading and revising.
1812 Clark, George S. R. Kitson. *The English inheritance.* 1950. Includes an essay on the general influence of religion in the nineteenth century.
1813 Clark, Henry W. *History of English nonconformity.* 1911–13, 2 vols.
1814 Clarke, William K. Lowther. *A history of the S.P.C.K.* 1959.
1815 Cockshut, Anthony O. J. *Anglican attitudes: a study of Victorian religious controversies.* 1959. A pleasant sketch.
1816 —— *The unbelievers: English agnostic thought 1840–1890.* 1964.
1817 Collier, Richard. *The general next to God: the story of William Booth and the Salvation Army.* 1965.
1818 Coulson, John and Arthur M. Allchin (eds.). *The rediscovery of Newman: an Oxford symposium.* 1967.
1819 Dale, Robert W. *History of English Congregationalism,* ed. Sir Alfred W. W. Dale. 2nd ed., 1907.
1820 Davies, Ebenezer T. *Religion in the industrial revolution in South Wales.* Cardiff, 1965.

1821 Davies, Horton. *Worship and theology in England*, III, *From Watts and Wesley to Maurice, 1690–1850*, IV, *From Newman to Martineau, 1850–1900*. Princeton, 1961–2. A massive survey of comparative liturgical history.

1822 Davies, Walter M. *An introduction to F. D. Maurice's theology; based on the first edition of The kingdom of Christ (1838) and The faith of the liturgy and the doctrine of the thirty-nine articles (1860)*. 1964.

1823 Elliott-Binns, Leonard E. *The development of English theology in the later nineteenth century*. 1952.

1824 —— *English thought, 1860–1900: the theological aspect*. 1956.

1825 Escott, Harry. *A history of Scottish congregationalism*. Glasgow, 1960.

1826 Faber, Geoffrey. *Oxford apostles: a character study of the Oxford movement*. 2nd ed., 1936. An analysis of the leading figures, refreshingly free from the odour of sanctity.

1827 Faulkner, Harold U. *Chartism and the churches*. New York, 1916.

1828 Fitzsimons, John (ed.). *Manning: Anglican and Catholic*. 1951.

1829 Fleming, John R. *A history of the Church in Scotland, 1843–1874*. Edinburgh, 1927.

1830 Fries, Heinrich and Werner Becker (eds.). *Newman Studien*. Nürnberg, 1948–.

1831 Gillow, Joseph. *A literary and biographical history, or bibliographical dictionary of the English Catholics* . . . 1885–1903, 5 vols.

1832 Glover, Willis B. *Evangelical nonconformists and higher criticism in the nineteenth century*. 1954.

1833 Gorman, W. Gordon. *Converts to Rome. A biographical list of the most notable converts to the Catholic Church in the United Kingdom during the last sixty years*. New ed., 1910.

1834 Grant, John W. *Free churchmanship in England, 1870–1940*. 1955. With special reference to Congregationalism.

1835 Green, Vivian H. H. *Religion at Oxford and Cambridge*. 1964.

1836 Grønbech, Vilhelm P. *Religious currents in the nineteenth century*, tr. Phillip M. Mitchell and William D. Paden. Lawrence, Kans., 1965. Originally published 1922; discusses Tennyson, Darwin and Newman.

1837 Gwynn, Denis R. *A hundred years of Catholic emancipation 1829–1929*. 1929.

1838 Hall, Trevor H. *The spiritualists: the story of Florence Cook and William Crookes*. 1962.

1839 Härdelin, Alf. *The tractarian understanding of the eucharist*. Uppsala, 1965.

1840 Harrison, Archibald W., B. Aquila Barber, George C. Hornby and E. Tegla Davies. *The Methodist Church: its origin, divisions, and re-union*. 1932.

1841 Harrold, Charles F. *John Henry Newman; an expository and critical study of his mind, thought and art*. 1945.

1842 Heasman, Kathleen. *Evangelicals in action; an appraisal of their social work in the Victorian era*. 1962.

1843 Holt, Raymond V. *The Unitarian contribution to social progress in England*. 2nd ed., 1952.

1844 Hurst, John F. *The history of methodism*, III. 1901.

1845 Inglis, Kenneth S. *Churches and the working class in Victorian England*. 1963. A major study of the failure of the churches.

1846 *John Henry Newman: centenary essays*. 1945.

1847 Jones, Peter d'A. *The Christian socialist revival, 1877–1914: religion, class, and social conscience in late-Victorian England*. Princeton, 1968.

1848 Jones, Rufus M. *The later periods of Quakerism*, III. 1921.

1849 Kellett, Ernest E. *Religion and life in the early Victorian age*. 1938.

1850 Kendall, Holliday B. *History of the Primitive Methodist Church*. Rev. ed., 1919.

1851 Kent, John. *The age of disunity*. 1966. A study of nineteenth-century Methodism.

1852 Lack, David L. *Evolutionary theory and Christian belief: the unresolved conflict*. 1957.

1853 Lipman, Vivian D. (ed.). *Three centuries of Anglo-Jewish history*. 1961.

1854 Lochhead, Marion. *Episcopal Scotland in the nineteenth century.* 1966.
1855 McClatchey, Diana. *Oxfordshire clergy 1777–1869.* Oxford, 1960.
1856 McDonald, Hugh D. *Ideas of revelation: an historical study A.D. 1700 to A.D. 1860.* 1959.
1857 —— *Theories of revelation: an historical study, 1860–1960.* 1963.
1858 MacDougall, Hugh A. *The Acton–Newman relations: the dilemma of Christian liberalism.* New York, 1962.
1859 McElrath, Damian. *The Syllabus of Pius IX: some reactions in England.* Louvain, 1964.
1860 McEntee, Georgiana P. *The social Catholic movement in Great Britain.* New York, 1927.
1861 McGee, John E. *History of the British secular movement.* Girard, Kans., 1948.
1862 Manning, Bernard L. *The Protestant dissenting deputies.* Cambridge, 1952.
1863 Marlowe, John (pseud.). *The puritan tradition in English life.* 1957.
1864 Martin, Hugh (ed.). *Christian social reformers of the nineteenth century.* 1927.
1865 Mayor, Stephen. *The churches and the labour movement.* 1967.
1866 Mechie, Stewart. *The Church and Scottish social development, 1780–1870.* 1960.
1867 Moule, Handley C. G. *The evangelical school in the Church of England: its men and its work in the nineteenth century.* 1901.
1868 Neill, Stephen. *The interpretation of the New Testament, 1861–1961.* 1964.
1869 Newsome, David. *Godliness and good learning: four studies on a Victorian ideal.* 1961. The public schools and the transformation from 'godliness and good learning' to 'muscular Christianity'.
1870 Nias, John C. S. *Gorham and the Bishop of Exeter.* 1951.
1871 Norman, Edward R. *Anti-catholicism in Victorian England* (Historical Problems: Studies and Documents, 1). 1968.
1872 —— *The Catholic Church and Ireland in the age of rebellion, 1859–1873.* 1965. Useful for political history.
1873 O'Connor, John J. *The Catholic revival in England.* New York, 1942.
1874 Orr, J. Edwin. *The second evangelical awakening in Britain.* 1949. The revival of 1859.
1875 Payne, Ernest A. *The Baptist Union; a short history.* 1959.
1876 Peck, William G. *The social implications of the Oxford movement.* 1933.
1877 Peel, Albert. *These hundred years. A history of the Congregational Union of England and Wales, 1831–1931.* 1931.
1878 Phillips, Walter A. (ed.). *History of the Church of Ireland, from the earliest times to the present day,* III, *The modern Church.* Oxford, 1933.
1879 Pollock, John C. *A Cambridge movement.* 1953. The Cambridge Inter-collegiate Christian Union.
1880 Port, Michael. *Six hundred new churches; a study of the Church Building Commission, 1818–1856, and its church building activities.* 1961.
1881 Ramsey, Arthur M. *F. D. Maurice and the conflicts of modern theology.* Cambridge, 1951.
1882 Raven, Charles E. *Christian socialism, 1848–1854.* 1920.
1883 Reckitt, Maurice B. *Maurice to Temple: a century of the social movement in the Church of England.* 1947.
1884 Reynolds, John S. *The evangelicals at Oxford, 1735–1871; a record of an unchronicled movement.* Oxford, 1953.
1885 Robertson, John M. *A history of freethought in the nineteenth century.* 1929, 2 vols.
1886 Rodgers, John H. *The theology of P. T. Forsyth: the cross of Christ and the revelation of God.* 1965.
1887 Roth, Cecil A. *Essays and portraits in Anglo-Jewish history.* Philadelphia, 1962.
1888 —— *A history of the Jews in England.* 2nd ed., Oxford, 1949. The standard history.
1889 Sandall, Robert. *The history of the Salvation Army,* completed by Arch R. Wiggins. 1947–64, 4 vols. The official history.
1890 Sanders, Charles R. *Coleridge and the broad church movement; studies in S. T. Coleridge, Dr. Arnold of Rugby, J. C. Hare, Thomas Carlyle and F. D. Maurice.* Durham, N.C., 1942.
1891 Shaw, Thomas. *The Bible Christians, 1815–1907.* 1965.

1892   Simpson, William J. Sparrow. *The history of the Anglo-Catholic revival from 1845.* 1932.
1893   Smith, Henry, John E. Swallow and William Treffry (eds.). *The story of the United Methodist Church.* 1932.
1894   Smith, Warren S. *The London heretics, 1870–1914.* 1967. Non-Christian sects.
1895   Stephenson, Alan M. G. *The first Lambeth conference, 1867.* 1967.
1896   Stewart, Herbert L. *A century of Anglo-Catholicism.* 1929.
1897   Stock, Eugene. *The history of the Church Missionary Society, its environment, its men and its work.* 1899–1916, 3 vols.
1898   Storr, Vernon F. *Freedom and tradition: a study of liberal evangelicalism.* 1940.
1899   Sykes, Christopher. *Two studies in virtue.* 1953. The first study deals with Richard Waldo Sibthorp.
1900   Sykes, John. *The Quakers.* 1959.
1901   Sykes, Norman. *The English religious tradition.* 1953.
1902   Thureau-Dangin, Paul. *The English Catholic revival in the nineteenth century,* tr. Wilfrid Wilberforce. 1914, 2 vols. Treats both Roman and Anglo-Catholicism.
1903   Tierney, Michael (ed.). *Struggle with fortune, a miscellany for the centenary of the Catholic University of Ireland, 1854–1954.* Dublin, 1954.
1904   Townsend, William J., Herbert B. Workman and George Eayrs (eds.). *A new history of Methodism,* I. 1909.
1905   Tribe, David. *100 years of free thought.* 1967.
1906   Tulloch, John. *Movements of religious thought in Britain during the nineteenth century.* 1885.
1907   Vidler, Alec R. *F. D. Maurice and company: nineteenth century studies.* 2nd ed., 1966.
1908   —— *The theology of F. D. Maurice.* 1948.
1909   Voll, Dieter. *Catholic evangelicalism: the acceptance of evangelical traditions by the Oxford movement during the second half of the nineteenth century,* tr. Veronica Ruffer. 1963.
1910   Wagner, Donald O. *The Church of England and social reform since 1854.* 1930.
1911   Walgrave, Jan H. *Newman the theologian; the nature of belief and doctrine as exemplified in his life and works,* tr. Arthur V. Littledale. 1960.
1912   Ward, Bernard. *The sequel to Catholic emancipation, 1830–1850.* 1913–15, 2 vols.
1913   Watson, Bernard. *A hundred years' war: the Salvation Army, 1865–1965.* 1965.
1914   Wearmouth, Robert F. *Methodism and the struggle of the working classes 1850–1900.* Leicester, 1955. May exaggerate the influence of Methodism.
1915   —— *Methodism and the working-class movements of England 1800–1850.* 1937.
1916   Webb, Clement C. J. *A study of religious thought in England from 1850.* Oxford, 1933.
1917   Whitley, William T. *A history of British Baptists.* 2nd ed., 1932.
1918   Wickham, Edward R. *Church and people in an industrial city.* 1957. The negligible influence of the Church in Sheffield.
1919   Wilkinson, John T. *1662 and after: three centuries of English nonconformity.* 1962.
1920   Wood, Herbert G. *Belief and unbelief since 1850.* Cambridge, 1955.

4 Biographies

1921   Abercrombie, Nigel. *The life and work of Edmund Bishop.* 1960.
1922   Ashwell, Arthur R. and Reginald G. Wilberforce. *Life of the Right Reverend Samuel Wilberforce, D.D., Lord Bishop of Oxford and afterwards of Winchester, with selections from his diaries and correspondence.* Rev. ed., 1888, 3 vols.
1923   Bamford, Thomas W. *Thomas Arnold.* 1960.
1924   Barnett, Henrietta O. W. *Canon Barnett, his life, work, and friends.* 1918, 2 vols. Life of a leader in the settlement movement, by his wife.

1925 Battiscombe, Georgina. *John Keble: a study in limitations.* 1963. A good spiritual biography.

1926 Begbie, Harold. *Life of William Booth, the founder of the Salvation Army.* 1920.

1927 Bell, George K. A. *Randall Davidson, Archbishop of Canterbury.* 3rd ed., 1952.

1928 Bennett, Frederick. *The story of W. J. E. Bennett.* 1909.

1929 Benson, Arthur C. *The life of Edward White Benson.* 1899, 2 vols.

1930 Bettany, Frederick G. *Stewart Headlam: a biography.* 1926.

1931 Blomfield, Alfred. *A memoir of Charles James Blomfield.* 1863, 2 vols. Still the only biography of the great bishop of London.

1932 Bouyer, Louis. *Newman: his life and spirituality,* tr. J. Lewis May. 1958. Despite the hagiographic bias, this is the best one-volume biography.

1933 Brandreth, Henry R. T. *Dr. Lee of Lambeth: a chapter in parenthesis in the history of the Oxford movement.* 1951. On the movement for corporate reunion.

1934 Bromley, John. *The man of ten talents: a portrait of Richard Chenevix Trench, 1807–1886: philologist, poet, theologian, archbishop.* 1959.

1935 Bunting, Thomas P. *The life of Jabez Bunting, D.D., with notices of contemporary persons and events.* 1859–87, 2 vols.

1936 Burgon, John W. *Lives of twelve good men.* New ed., 1891, 2 vols. The good men are Routh, Rose, Marriott, Hawkins, Samuel Wilberforce, Cotton, Greswell, Coxe, Mansel and Jacobson.

1937 Butler, Dom Cuthbert. *The life and times of Bishop Ullathorne.* 1926, 2 vols. The best of the older Catholic biographies.

1938 Butterfield, Herbert. *Lord Acton* (Historical Association, General Series, IX). 1948. A brief appraisal.

1939 Carlile, John C. *C. H. Spurgeon, an interpretative biography.* 1933.

1940 Carpenter, James. *Gore: a study in liberal Catholic thought.* 1960.

1941 Chapman, Ronald. *Father Faber.* 1961. Important for its critical treatment of Newman.

1942 Church, Mary C. *Life and letters of Dean Church.* 1895.

1943 Dale, Alfred W. W. *The life of R. W. Dale of Birmingham.* 1898.

1944 Davidson, Randall T. and William Benham. *Life of Archibald Campbell Tait, Archbishop of Canterbury.* 1891, 2 vols.

1945 Davies, George C. B. *Henry Phillpotts: Bishop of Exeter 1778–1869.* 1954.

1946 Dessain, Charles Stephen. *John Henry Newman.* 1966. A short biography by an expert.

1947 Drummond, James and Charles B. Upton. *The life and letters of James Martineau.* 1902, 2 vols.

1948 Elton, Godfrey, Baron. *Edward King and our times.* 1958. A judgment of the controversial Bishop of Lincoln.

1949 Ernle, Rowland E. Prothero, Baron and George G. Bradley. *The life and correspondence of Arthur Penrhyn Stanley, D.D., late Dean of Westminster.* 1893, 2 vols.

1950 Ervine, St John G. *God's soldier: General William Booth.* 1934, 2 vols.

1951 Fallows, William G. *Mandell Creighton and the English Church.* 1964.

1952 Fothergill, Brian. *Nicholas Wiseman.* 1963.

1953 Gill, John C. *Parson Bull of Byerley.* 1963.

1954 —— *The ten hours parson; Christian social action in the eighteen-thirties.* 1959. Also on George S. Bull.

1955 Gruber, Jacob W. *A conscience in conflict: the life of St George Jackson Mivart.* Philadelphia, 1960. Also relevant to the history of science.

1956 Hanna, William. *Memoirs of the life and writings of Thomas Chalmers, D.D.* New ed., Edinburgh, 1878, 2 vols.

1957 Herford, Charles H. *Philip Henry Wicksteed, his life and work.* 1931. On the 'Labour Church'.

1958 Higham, Florence. *Frederick Denison Maurice.* 1947.

1959 Himmelfarb, Gertrude. *Lord Acton: a study in conscience and politics.* Chicago, 1952. The first biography, but new documents and monographs make revision imperative.

1960 Hinchcliff, Peter. *John William Colenso, Bishop of Natal.* 1964.
1961 Hughes, Dorothea Price. *The life of Hugh Price Hughes.* 1904.
1962 Johnston, John O. *Life and letters of Henry Parry Liddon, D.D., D.C.L., Ll.D., Canon of St. Paul's Cathedral, and sometime Ireland Professor of Exegesis in the University of Oxford.* 1904.
1963 Kent, John. *Jabez Bunting, the last Wesleyan. A study in the Methodist ministry after the death of John Wesley.* 1955.
1964 Kingsley, Frances E. (ed.). *Charles Kingsley, his letters and memories of his life.* 1877, 2 vols.
1965 Kirk-Smith, Harold. *William Thomson, Archbishop of York; his life and times, 1819–90.* 1958.
1966 Leetham, Claude R. *Luigi Gentili: a sower for the second spring.* 1966.
1967 Leslie, Shane. *Henry Edward Manning: his life and labours.* 1921. Highly favourable to Manning as a Catholic; a corrective to (1983).
1968 Liddon, Henry P. *Life of Edward Bouverie Pusey, Doctor of Divinity, Canon of Christ Church, Regius Professor of Hebrew in the University of Oxford,* ed. John O. Johnston and Robert J. Wilson. 1893–7, 4 vols.
1969 Longden, Henry I. *Northampton and Rutland clergy, A.D. 1500–1900.* Northampton, 1939–52, 16 vols. Biographical dictionary of hundreds of clergy.
1970 McClelland, Vincent A. *Cardinal Manning, his public life and influence, 1865–1892.* 1962. Limited to the public activities of Manning's archbishopric.
1971 McCormack, Arthur. *Cardinal Vaughan: the life of the third Archbishop of Westminster.* 1966.
1972 MacSuibhne, Peadar. *Paul Cullen and his contemporaries, with their letters from 1820 to 1902.* Naas, 1961–5, 3 vols. Not a critical biography of the Irish cardinal.
1973 Marchant, James. *Dr. John Clifford, C.H.: life, letters, and reminiscences.* 1924. Life of a leading Baptist minister.
1974 Martin, Robert B. *The dust of combat, a life of Charles Kingsley.* 1960.
1975 Masterman, Neville C. *John Malcolm Ludlow: the builder of Christian socialism.* Cambridge, 1963.
1976 Maurice, John F. *The life of Frederick Denison Maurice.* 1884, 2 vols.
1977 Miall, Arthur. *Life of Edward Miall.* 1884.
1978 Newsome, David. *The parting of friends: the Wilberforces and Henry Manning.* 1966. This composite biography is a model of biographical history. American ed. inverts title and subtitle.
1979 Overton, John H. and Elizabeth Wordsworth. *Christopher Wordsworth, Bishop of Lincoln, 1807–1885.* New ed., 1890.
1980 Paget, Stephen (ed.). *Henry Scott Holland . . . Regius Professor of Divinity in Oxford, Canon of St. Paul's: memoir and letters.* 1921.
1981 Pope-Hennessy, Una. *Canon Charles Kingsley; a biography.* 1948.
1982 Prestige, George L. *The life of Charles Gore, a great Englishman.* 1935.
1983 Purcell, Edmund S. *Life of Cardinal Manning, Archbishop of Westminster.* 1896, 2 vols. A thoroughly bad biography, but indispensable for the letters which it preserved; the basis of the errors in (1994).
1984 Reynolds, Ernest E. *Three cardinals: Newman, Wiseman, Manning.* 1958.
1985 Reynolds, Michael. *Martyr of ritualism: Father Mackonochie of St. Alban's, Holborn.* 1965.
1986 Robbins, William. *The Newman brothers: an essay in comparative intellectual biography.* 1966. Good religious and intellectual history.
1987 Rogers, Patrick. *Father Theobald Mathew: apostle of temperance.* Dublin, 1943.
1988 Russell, George W. E. *Edward King, sixtieth Bishop of Lincoln.* 1912. An official biography.
1989 Sandford, Ernest G. *Memoirs of Archbishop Temple, by seven friends.* 1906, 2 vols.
1990 Smith, Basil A. *Dean Church, the Anglican response to Newman.* 1958.
1991 Snead-Cox, John G. *The life of Cardinal Vaughan.* 1910, 2 vols.
1992 Stanley, Arthur P. *The life and correspondence of Thomas Arnold.* 1877, 2 vols.

1993 Stephens, William R. W. *The life and letters of Walter Farquhar Hook*, *D.D.*, *F.R.S.* 6th ed., 1881.
1994 Strachey, G. Lytton. *Eminent Victorians: Cardinal Manning, Florence Nightingale, Dr. Arnold, General Gordon.* 1928. Brilliantly malicious sketches, admirably representative of the anti-Victorian temper of the 1920s.
1995 Sumner, George H. *Life of Charles Richard Sumner, D.D., Bishop of Winchester, during a forty years' episcopate.* 1876.
1996 Thirlwall, John Connop. *Connop Thirlwall, historian and theologian.* 1936.
1997 Trevor, Meriol. *Newman, light in winter.* 1962.
1998 —— *Newman, the pillar of the cloud.* 1962. These two volumes are beautifully written, minutely detailed, uncritical hagiography.
1999 Ward, Maisie. *The Wilfrid Wards and the transition*, I, *the nineteenth century.* 1934. A pleasant sketch by their daughter.
2000 Ward, Wilfrid. *The life and times of Cardinal Wiseman.* 1897, 2 vols. Useful for the Catholic revival.
2001 —— *The life of John Henry Cardinal Newman.* 1912, 2 vols. Still standard for the Catholic period.
2002 —— *William George Ward and the Catholic revival.* 2nd ed., 1912. By his son, the most eminent of Catholic biographers.
2003 —— *William George Ward and the Oxford movement.* 2nd ed., 1890.
2004 Webster, Alan B. *Joshua Watson; the story of a layman, 1771–1855.* 1954. Lay activity in the Church of England.
2005 Westcott, Arthur. *Life and letters of Brooke Foss Westcott, D.D., D.C.L., sometime Bishop of Durham.* 1903, 2 vols.
2006 Williams, Thomas J. *Priscilla Lydia Sellon: the restorer after three centuries of the religious life in the English Church.* 1966.
2007 Wood, Herbert G. *Frederick Denison Maurice.* Cambridge, 1950.
2008 Wymer, Norman. *Dr. Arnold of Rugby.* 1953. A popular modern treatment.

5 Articles

2009 Ahern, John. 'The plenary synod of Thurles', *Irish Ecclesiastical Record*, **75** (Nov. 1951), 395–403; **78** (July 1952), 1–20.
2010 Altholz, Josef L. 'Gladstone and the Vatican decrees', *The Historian*, **25** (May 1963), 312–24.
2011 —— 'Newman and history', *VS*, **7** (Mar. 1964), 285–94. See also the reply by Derek Holmes, *VS*, **8** (Mar. 1965), 271–7.
2012 Anderson, Olive. 'The reactions of church and dissent towards the Crimean war', *JEH*, **16** (Oct. 1965), 209–20.
2013 Ausubel, Herman. 'General Booth's scheme of social salvation', *AHR*, **56** (Apr. 1951), 519–25.
2014 Backstrom, Philip N., Jr. 'The practical side of Christian socialism in Victorian England', *VS*, **6** (June 1963), 305–24.
2015 Bahlman, Dudley W. R. 'The Queen, Mr. Gladstone, and Church patronage', *VS*, **3** (June 1960), 349–80.
2016 Best, Geoffrey F. A. 'Popular Protestantism in Victorian England', in *Id. & Inst.*, pp. 115–42. A major contribution.
2017 —— 'The religious difficulties of national education in England, 1800–70', *Camb. Hist. J.*, **12** (no. 2, 1956), 155–73.
2018 Blehl, Vincent F. 'Newman and the missing miter', *Thought*, **35** (Spring 1960), 110–23.
2019 Brose, Olive J. 'F. D. Maurice and the Victorian crisis of belief', *VS*, **3** (Mar. 1960), 227–48.
2020 Budd, Susan. 'The loss of faith: reasons for unbelief among members of the secular movement in England, 1850–1950', *PP*, **36** (Apr. 1967), 106–25.
2021 Butterfield, Herbert. 'Acton: his training, methods and intellectual system', in Arshag O. Sarkissian (ed.). *Studies in diplomatic history and historiography in honour of G. P. Gooch, C.H.* 1961, pp. 161–98.

2022 Cahill, Gilbert A. 'The Protestant Association and the anti-Maynooth agitation of 1845', *Catholic Historical Review*, **43** (Oct. 1957), 273–308.

2023 Charles, Conrad. 'The origins of the parish mission in England and the early Passionist apostolate, 1840–1850', *JEH*, **15** (Apr. 1964), 60–75.

2024 Clegg, Herbert. 'Evangelicals and tractarians', *Historical Magazine of the Protestant Episcopal Church*, **35** (June 1966), 111–53 (Sept. 1966), 237–94; **36** (June 1967), 127–78.

2025 DeLaura, David J. 'Matthew Arnold and John Henry Newman: the "Oxford sentiment" and the religion of the future', *Texas Studies in Literature and Language*, **6** (Supplement, 1965), 573–702. Traces the connexions and shows that Newman was almost essential to Arnold's growth.

2026 Dell, Robert S. 'Social and economic theories and pastoral concerns of a Victorian archbishop', *JEH*, **16** (Oct. 1965), 196–208. The archbishop is J. B. Sumner.

2027 Erickson, Arvel B. 'The non-intrusion controversy in Scotland, 1832–1843', *Church History*, **11** (Dec. 1942), 302–25.

2028 Eros, John. 'The rise of organised freethought in mid-Victorian England', *Sociological Review*, new ser., **2** (July 1954), 98–120.

2029 Flindall, R. P. 'The parish priest in Victorian England', *CQR*, **168** (July–Sept. 1967), 296–306.

2030 Fulweiler, Howard W. 'Tractarians and philistines: the *Tracts for the Times* versus Victorian middle-class values', *Historical Magazine of the Protestant Episcopal Church*, **31** (Mar. 1962), 36–53.

2031 Greene, John C. 'Darwin and religion', in Harlow Shapley (ed.). *Science ponders religion*. New York, 1960, pp. 254–76.

2032 Harrison, Brian. 'Religion and recreation in nineteenth-century England', *PP*, **38** (Dec. 1967), 98–125.

2033 Hinchcliff, Peter. 'John William Colenso: a fresh appraisal', *JEH*, **13** (Oct. 1962), 203–16.

2034 Holmes, J. Derek. 'Cardinal Newman and the Affirmation Bill', *Historical Magazine of the Protestant Episcopal Church*, **36** (Mar. 1967), 87–97.

2035 —— 'Newman, Froude and Pattison: some aspects of their relations', *Journal of Religious History*, **4** (June 1966), 28–38.

2036 Ingham, S. M. 'The disestablishment movement in England 1868–74', *Journal of Religious History*, **3** (June 1964), 38–60.

2037 Inglis, Kenneth S. 'English nonconformity and social reform, 1880–1900', *PP*, **13** (Apr. 1958), 73–88.

2038 —— 'The Labour Church movement', *IRSH*, **3** (pt. 3, 1958), 445–60.

2039 —— 'Patterns of religious worship in 1851', *JEH*, **11** (Apr. 1960), 74–86. On the method of the 1851 census and its results in large towns.

2040 Kent, John. 'Hugh Price Hughes and the nonconformist conscience', in Gareth V. Bennett and J. D. Walsh (eds.). *Essays in modern English church history in memory of Norman Sykes*. 1966, pp. 181–205.

2041 Larkin, Emmet. 'Church and state in Ireland in the nineteenth century', *Church History*, **31** (Sept. 1962), 294–306.

2042 —— 'Economic growth, capital investment, and the Roman Catholic Church in nineteenth-century Ireland', *AHR*, **72** (Apr. 1967), 852–84. A pioneering study of church finances and their repercussions.

2043 Machin, George I. T. 'The Maynooth grant, the dissenters and disestablishment, 1845–1847', *EHR*, **82** (Jan. 1967), 61–85.

2044 McClelland, Vincent A. 'The Irish clergy and Archbishop Manning's apostolic visitation of the western district of Scotland, 1867', *Catholic Historical Review*, **53** (Apr. 1967), 1–27; (July 1967), 229–50.

2045 —— 'The Protestant Alliance and Roman Catholic schools, 1872–74', *VS*, **8** (Dec. 1964), 173–82.

2046 McElrath, Damian. 'Richard Simpson and John Henry Newman: the *Rambler*, laymen, and theology', *Catholic Historical Review*, **52** (Jan. 1967), 509–33.

2047 MacLaren, A. Allan. 'Presbyterianism and the working class in a mid-nineteenth century city', *SHR*, **46** (Oct. 1967), 115–39. The case of Aberdeen.

2048 Mandelbaum, Maurice. 'Darwin's religious views', *JHI*, **19** (June 1958), 363–78.

2049 Marsh, Peter T. 'The primate and the prime minister: Archbishop Tait, Gladstone, and the national Church', *VS*, **9** (Dec. 1965), 113–40.

2050 Meacham, Standish. 'The Church in the Victorian city', *VS*, **11** (Mar. 1968), 359–78.

2051 —— 'The evangelical inheritance', *JBS*, **3** (Nov. 1963), 88–104. A perceptive treatment of the later generations of evangelicals.

2052 Mole, David E. H. 'John Cale Miller: a Victorian rector of Birmingham', *JEH*, **17** (Apr. 1966), 95–103.

2053 Murphy, Howard R. 'The ethical revolt against Christian orthodoxy in early Victorian England', *AHR*, **60** (July 1955), 800–17. A valuable new approach to the decline of orthodoxy.

2054 Newsome, David H. 'The churchmanship of Samuel Wilberforce', in Geoffrey J. Cuming (ed.). *Studies in church history*, III. Leiden, 1966, pp. 23–47.

2055 Norman, Edward R. 'The Maynooth question of 1845', *IHS*, **15** (Sept. 1967), 407–37.

2056 Nurser, John S. 'The religious conscience in Lord Acton's political thought', *JHI*, **22** (Jan.–Mar. 1961), 47–62.

2057 Pickering, W. S. F. 'The 1851 religious census—a useless experiment?', *British Journal of Sociology*, **18** (Dec. 1967), 382–407.

2058 Pierson, Stanley. 'John Trevor and the Labour Church movement in England, 1891–1900', *Church History*, **29** (Dec. 1960), 463–78.

2059 Pinnington, John E. 'Bishop Blomfield and St. Barnabas, Pimlico: the limits of ecclesiastical authority', *CQR*, **168** (July–Sept. 1967), 289–96.

2060 Rayner, K. 'The home base of the missions of the Church of England 1830–50', *Journal of Religious History*, **2** (June 1962), 29–48.

2061 St John-Stevas, Norman. 'The Victorian conscience: an assessment and explanation', *Wiseman Review*, **236** (Autumn 1962), 247–59.

2062 Sellars, Ian. 'Unitarians and social change', *Hibbert Journal*, **61** (Jan., Apr., July 1963), 76–80, 122–7, 177–80.

2063 Shannon, Richard T. 'John Robert Seeley and the idea of a national church', in *Id. & Inst.*, pp. 236–67.

2064 Smith, Francis B. 'The atheist mission, 1840–1900', in *Id. & Inst.*, pp. 205–35.

2065 Stephen, M. D. 'Gladstone's ecclesiastical patronage, 1868–1874', *Historical Studies, Australia and New Zealand*, **11** (Apr. 1964), 145–62.

2066 —— 'Liberty, Church and state: Gladstone's relations with Manning and Acton, 1832–70', *Journal of Religious History*, **1** (Dec. 1961), 217–32.

2067 Thompson, David M. 'The 1851 religious census: problems and possibilities', *VS*, **11** (Sept. 1967), 87–97. Emphasis on the East Midlands.

2068 Vale, Mary. 'Origins of the Catholic University of Ireland, 1845–1854', *Irish Ecclesiastical Record*, **82** (July, Sept., Oct. 1954), 1–16, 152–62, 226–41.

2069 Walker, R. B. 'Religious change in Cheshire, 1750–1850', *JEH*, **17** (Apr. 1966), 77–94.

2070 Welch, P. J. 'Blomfield and Peel: a study in co-operation between Church and state, 1841–1846', *JEH*, **12** (Apr. 1961), 71–84.

2071 Welsby, Paul A. 'Church and people in Victorian Ipswich', *CQR*, **164** (Apr.–June 1963), 207–17.

2072 Whyte, John H. 'The appointment of Catholic bishops in nineteenth century Ireland', *Catholic Historical Review*, **48** (Apr. 1962), 12–32.

2073 Winn, William E. '*Tom Brown's School Days* and the development of "muscular Christianity"', *Church History*, **29** (Mar. 1960), 64–73.

XIII HISTORY OF THE FINE ARTS

1 Printed sources

2074 Doughty, Oswald and John R. Wahl (eds.). *Letters of Dante Gabriel Rossetti*. Oxford, 1965–7, 4 vols. Index volume still to be published.
2075 Pope, Willard B. (ed.). *The diary of Benjamin Robert Haydon*. 1960–3, 5 vols.
2076 Rossetti, William M. (ed.). *Praeraphaelite diaries and letters*. 1900. Rossetti correspondence 1835–54, F. M. Brown's diary 1844–56, *PRB* journal kept by Rossetti 1849–53.
2077 Ruskin, John. *Modern painters: their superiority in the art of landscape painting to all the ancient masters proved . . . from the works of modern artists, especially from those of J. M. W. Turner, Esq., R.A.* 1843–60, 5 vols.

2 Surveys

2078 Bertram, Anthony. *A century of British painting, 1851–1951.* 1951.
2079 Boase, Thomas S. R. *English art, 1800–1870* (Oxford History of English Art, x). Oxford, 1959. Extensive bibliographies. Vol. xi in this excellent series has not yet appeared.
2080 Casson, Hugh M. *An introduction to Victorian architecture.* 1948.
2081 Colles, Henry C. *Symphony and drama, 1850–1900* (The Oxford History of Music, vii). 1934.
2082 Dannreuther, Edward. *The Romantic period* (The Oxford History of Music, vi). 1931.
2083 Gaunt, William. *A concise history of English painting.* 1964.
2084 Goodhart-Rendel, Harry S. *English architecture since the regency: an interpretation.* 1953.
2085 Grove, George. *Dictionary of music and musicians.* 5th ed., ed. Eric Blom, 1954, 9 vols. Indispensable.
2086 Hitchcock, Henry-Russell. *Architecture: nineteenth and twentieth centuries* (Pelican History of Art, xv). Harmondsworth, 1958. A general survey by the leading authority.
2087 Hubbard, Hesketh. *A hundred years of British painting 1851–1951.* 1951.
2088 Jordan, Robert F. *Victorian architecture.* 1966.
2089 Kidson, Peter and Peter Murray. *A history of English architecture.* 1962.
2090 Reynolds, Graham. *Victorian painting.* 1966.
2091 Turnor, C. Reginald. *Nineteenth century architecture in Britain.* 1950.
2092 Walker, Ernest. *A history of music in England.* 3rd ed. revised by Jack A. Westrup. Oxford, 1952. The standard general survey.

3 Monographs

2093 Ames, Winslow. *Prince Albert and Victorian taste.* 1967.
2094 Barman, Christian A. *An introduction to railway architecture.* 1950.
2095 Bell, Quentin. *The schools of design.* 1963. State-aided schools.
2096 —— *Victorian artists.* 1967.
2097 Bemrose, Geoffrey. *Nineteenth century English pottery and porcelain.* 1952.
2098 Bøe, Alf. *From Gothic revival to functional form.* Oxford, 1957. Victorian theories of design.
2099 Briggs, Martin S. *The architect in history.* Oxford, 1927.
2100 —— *Puritan architecture and its future.* 1946.
2101 Caw, James L. *Scottish painting, past and present, 1620–1908.* Edinburgh, 1908.
2102 Chadwick, George F. *The works of Sir Joseph Paxton, 1803–1865.* 1961.
2103 Clark, Kenneth M. *The Gothic revival: an essay in the history of taste.* 2nd ed., 1950. The fundamental work on the subject.
2104 Clarke, Basil F. L. *Church builders of the nineteenth century: a study of the Gothic revival in England.* 1938.

2105 Collins, Peter. *Changing ideals in modern architecture, 1750–1950.* 1965.
2106 Cundall, Herbert M. *A history of British water colour painting.* Rev. ed., 1929.
2107 Davis, Frank. *Victorian patrons of the arts; twelve famous collections and their owners.* 1963.
2108 Edwards, Herbert C. R. and Leonard G. G. Ramsey (eds.). *The early Victorian period, 1830–1860* (Connoisseur Period Guides to the Houses, Decoration, Furnishing and Chattels of the Classic Periods, VI). 1958.
2109 Ferriday, Peter (ed.). *Victorian architecture.* 1963. A collection of essays.
2110 Fleming, Gordon H. *Rossetti and the Pre-Raphaelite Brotherhood.* 1967.
2111 Fuller-Maitland, John A. *The music of Parry and Stanford; an essay in comparative criticism.* Cambridge, 1934.
2112 Gaunt, William. *The Pre-Raphaelite dream.* 1965. A re-issue of *The Pre-Raphaelite tragedy.* 1942.
2113 —— *Victorian Olympus.* 1952. On the classical revival of the 1870s and 1880s.
2114 Gernsheim, Helmut. *Creative photography: aesthetic trends, 1839–1960.* 1962.
2115 —— *Masterpieces of Victorian photography.* 1951. A thorough account, illustrated.
2116 Gloag, John. *The English tradition in design.* New ed., 1960.
2117 —— *Victorian comfort. A social history of design from 1830 to 1900.* 1961.
2118 —— *Victorian taste: some social aspects of architecture and industrial design from 1820 to 1900.* 1962.
2119 Gloag, John and Derek Bridgwater. *A history of cast iron in architecture.* 1948.
2120 Godden, Geoffrey A. *Victorian Porcelain.* 1961.
2121 —— *British pottery and porcelain, 1780–1850.* 1964.
2122 Graves, Algernon. *A dictionary of artists who have exhibited works in the principal London exhibitions from 1760 to 1893.* 3rd ed., 1901.
2123 Gwynn, Denis. *Lord Shrewsbury, Pugin and the Catholic revival.* 1946. Gothic art and Roman Catholicism.
2124 Hitchcock, Henry-Russell. *Early Victorian architecture in Britain.* 1954, 2 vols. The best general review.
2125 Hubbard, Hesketh. *Some Victorian draughtsmen.* Cambridge, 1944.
2126 Hughes, George B. *Victorian pottery and porcelain.* 1959.
2127 Hughes, Gervase. *The music of Arthur Sullivan.* 1960.
2128 Hunt, W. Holman. *Pre-Raphaelitism and the Pre-Raphaelite Brotherhood.* 1905, 2 vols. By a survivor of the movement.
2129 Hutchings, Arthur. *Church music in the nineteenth century.* 1967.
2130 Ironside, Robin. *Pre-Raphaelite painters.* 1948.
2131 Kaye, Barrington. *The development of the architectural profession in Britain.* 1960.
2132 Kennedy, Michael. *The Hallé tradition: a century of music.* Manchester, 1960.
2133 Klingender, Francis D. *Art and the industrial revolution.* 1947. A Marxist interpretation.
2134 Lamb, Walter R. M. *The Royal Academy; a short history of its foundation and development.* Rev. ed., 1951.
2135 Lichten, Frances. *Decorative arts of Victoria's era.* New York, 1950.
2136 Lister, Raymond. *Victorian narrative paintings.* 1966.
2137 Mackerness, Eric D. *A social history of English music.* 1964.
2138 McLean, Ruari. *Victorian book design and colour printing.* 1963.
2139 Meeks, Carroll L. V. *The railroad station: an architectural history.* 1957.
2140 Pevsner, Nikolaus (ed.). *The buildings of England.* Harmondsworth, 1951–. A continuing series, by counties.
2141 Pevsner, Nikolaus. *High Victorian design.* 1951.
2142 Reynolds, Graham. *Painters of the Victorian scene.* 1953.
2143 Richards, James M. *The functional tradition in early industrial buildings.* 1958. Illustrated.
2144 Rosenthal, Harold. *Two centuries of opera at Covent Garden.* 1958.
2145 Scholes, Percy A. *The mirror of music, 1844–1944; a century of musical life in Britain as reflected in the pages of the Musical Times.* 1947, 2 vols.

2146 Spielmann, Marion H. *Millais and his works, with special reference to the exhibition at the Royal Academy, 1898.* 1898.
2147 Steegmann, John. *Consort of taste, 1830–1870.* 1950. On Prince Albert and changes in artistic taste.
2148 Stewart, Cecil. *The stones of Manchester.* 1956. A study of architecture and architects in nineteenth-century Manchester.
2149 Strasser, Alex. *Victorian photography.* New York, 1942.
2150 Thompson, A. Hamilton. *The English house* (Historical Association Pamphlets, 105). 1936. A good brief survey of domestic architecture.
2151 Toller, Jane. *Papier-maché in Great Britain and America.* 1962. Useful for this period.
2152 Wakefield, Hugh. *Victorian pottery.* 1962.
2153 Wardle, Patricia. *Victorian silver and silver-plate.* 1963.
2154 Welby, Thomas E. *The Victorian romantics 1850–70; the early work of Dante Gabriel Rossetti, William Morris, Burne-Jones, Swinburne, Simeon, Solomon, and their associates.* 1929. Art and poetry.
2155 Welland, Dennis S. R. *The Pre-Raphaelites in literature and art.* 1953.
2156 White, Eric W. *The rise of English opera.* 1951.
2157 White, James F. *The Cambridge movement: the ecclesiologists and the Gothic revival.* Cambridge, 1962. An important study.

4 Biographies

2158 Blunt, Wilfred. *Cockerell: Sydney Carlyle Cockerell, friend of Ruskin and William Morris and director of the Fitzwilliam Museum.* 1964.
2159 Burne-Jones, Georgiana. *Memorials of Edward Burne-Jones.* 2 vols., 1904.
2160 Carter, Harry. *Orlando Jewitt.* 1962. Life of a wood-engraver.
2161 Doughty, Oswald. *A Victorian romantic: Dante Gabriel Rossetti.* New ed., 1960. A study of the development of Rossetti's personality, not a critical evaluation of his work.
2162 Farr, Dennis L. A. *William Etty.* 1958.
2163 Finberg, Alexander J. *The life of J. M. W. Turner, R.A.* 2nd ed., 1961.
2164 George, Eric. *The life and death of Benjamin Robert Haydon, 1786–1846.* 1948.
2165 Graves, Charles L. *Hubert Parry, his life and works.* 1926.
2166 Greene, H. Plunket. *Charles Villiers Stanford.* 1935.
2167 Hussey, Christopher. *The life of Sir Edwin Lutyens.* 1950.
2168 Lindsay, Jack. *J. M. W. Turner: his life and work: a critical biography.* 1966.
2169 Lough, Arthur G. *The influence of John Mason Neale.* 1962.
2170 Millais, John G. *The life and letters of Sir John Everett Millais, president of the Royal Academy.* 3rd ed., 1902.
2171 Pearson, Hesketh. *Gilbert and Sullivan.* 1947.
2172 Rothenstein, John and Martin Butlin. *Turner.* 1964.
2173 Trappes-Lomax, Michael. *Pugin, a medieval Victorian.* 1932.
2174 Watts, Mary S. *George Frederick Watts: the annals of an artist's life.* 3 vols., 1912.
2175 Young, Percy M. (ed.). *Elgar, O.M.; a study of a musician.* 1955.

5 Articles

2176 Burd, Van Akin. 'Background to *Modern Painters:* the tradition and the Turner controversy', *PMLA*, **74** (June 1959), 254–67.
2177 —— 'Ruskin's defense of Turner: the imitative phase', *Philological Quarterly*, **37** (Oct. 1958), 465–83.
2178 Fox, Daniel M. 'Artists in the modern state: the nineteenth century background', *Journal of Aesthetics and Art Criticism*, **22** (Winter 1963), 135–48.
2179 Hitchcock, Henry-Russell. 'High Victorian Gothic', *VS*, **1** (Sept. 1957), 47–71.
2180 —— 'Late Victorian architecture, 1851–1900', *Royal Institute of British Architects Journal*, **44** (Oct. 1937), 1029–39.

2181 King, Anthony. 'George Godwin and the Art Union of London, 1837–1911', *VS*, **8** (Dec. 1964), 101–30.

2182 Maurer, Oscar. '*Punch* and the opera war, 1847–1867', *Texas Studies in Literature and Language*, **1** (Summer 1959), 139–70. Operatic rivalries as revealed by advertising and comment in *Punch*.

2183 Pevsner, Nikolaus. 'Art furniture of the eighteen-seventies', *Architectural Review*, **3** (Jan. 1952), 43–50.

2184 Rose, Elliot. 'The stone table in the Round Church and the crisis of the Cambridge Camden Society', *VS*, **10** (Dec. 1966), 119–44. A light-hearted treatment of the Cambridge ecclesiologists.

2185 Shenfield, Margaret. 'Shaw as a music critic', *Music & Letters*, **39** (Oct. 1958), 378–84.

2186 Temperley, Nicholas. 'The English romantic opera', *VS*, **9** (Mar. 1966), 293–301.

XIV INTELLECTUAL HISTORY

1 Printed sources

2187 Bury, John P. T. (ed.). *Romilly's Cambridge diary, 1832–42.* Cambridge, 1967. Diary of Joseph Romilly, registrary of Cambridge University.

2188 Elliot, Hugh S. R. (ed.). *The letters of John Stuart Mill.* 1910, 2 vols.

2189 Evans, Joan and John H. Whitehouse (eds.). *The diaries of John Ruskin.* Oxford, 1956–9, 3 vols.

2190 Fifoot, Cecil H. S. (ed.). *The letters of Frederic William Maitland.* 1965.

2191 Hayek, Friedrich August von (ed.). *John Stuart Mill and Harriet Taylor: their correspondence and subsequent marriage.* 1951. The introduction stresses the thesis of Harriet's influence over Mill. Cf. (2311).

2192 Henderson, Philip (ed.). *The letters of William Morris to his family and friends.* 1950. Important new material.

2193 Hutton, William H. (ed.). *Letters of William Stubbs, Bishop of Oxford, 1825–1901.* 1904.

2194 Hyde, Harford M. (ed.). *A Victorian historian: private letters of W. E. H. Lecky, 1859–1878.* 1947.

2195 Hyndman, Henry M. *The record of an adventurous life.* 1911. See also *Further reminiscences.* 1912.

2196 Laurence, Dan H. (ed.). *Bernard Shaw: collected letters,* I, *1874–1897.* 1965.

2197 Lowry, Howard F. (ed.). *The letters of Matthew Arnold to Arthur Hugh Clough.* 1932.

2198 Marshall, Alfred. *Principles of economics.* 9th (variorum) ed., ed. Claude W. Guillebaud. 1961, 2 vols.

2199 Mill, John Stuart. *Autobiography.* 1873.

2200 —— *Principles of political economy, with some of their applications to social philosophy,* ed. W. A. Ashley. 1909. A variorum edition, based on the 7th ed. (1871), noting all significant changes in previous editions.

2201 Mineka, Francis E. (ed.). *The earlier letters of John Stuart Mill, 1812–1848* (Collected Works of John Stuart Mill, XII–XIII). Toronto, 1963, 2 vols.

2202 Russell, Bertrand, 3rd Earl, and Patricia (eds.). *The Amberley papers: the letters and diaries of Lord and Lady Amberley.* 1937, 2 vols. The milieu of the 1870s; edited by their son.

2203 Russell, George W. E. (ed.). *Letters of Matthew Arnold 1848–1888.* New ed., 1901.

2204 Shaw, George Bernard *et al. Fabian essays.* 6th ed., 1962. With an introduction by Asa Briggs.

2205 Smiles, Samuel. *Self-help, with illustrations of conduct & perseverance,* ed. Asa Briggs. 1958.

2206 Stephen, Leslie (ed.). *Letters of John Richard Green.* 1901.

2207 Viljoen, Helen G. (ed.). *The Froude–Ruskin friendship, as represented through letters.* New York, 1967.
2208 Webb, Beatrice. *My apprenticeship.* 1926.

2 Surveys

2209 Barker, Ernest. *Political thought in England from 1848 to 1914.* 2nd ed., 1950.
2210 Brinton, Crane. *English political thought in the nineteenth century.* 2nd ed., Cambridge, Mass., 1949.
2211 Copleston, Frederick. *A history of philosophy,* VIII, *Bentham to Russell.* 1966.
2212 Ford, Boris (ed.). *From Dickens to Hardy* (Pelican Guide to English Literature, VI). 1958. Essays on literature, the arts and their background.
2213 Harrison, Wilfred. *Conflict and compromise: history of British political thought, 1593–1900.* New York, 1965.
2214 Merz, John T. *A history of European thought in the nineteenth century.* Edinburgh, 1896–1914, 4 vols.
2215 Metz, Rudolph. *A hundred years of British philosophy,* tr. John W. Harvey, Thomas E. Jessop and Henry Sturt, ed. John H. Muirhead. 1938.
2216 Passmore, John A. *A hundred years of philosophy.* 1957.
2217 Somervell, David C. *English thought in the nineteenth century.* 1929.
2218 Sorley, William R. *A history of British philosophy to 1900.* Rev. ed., Cambridge, 1965.
2219 Ward, Adolphus W. and Alfred R. Waller (eds.). *The Cambridge history of English literature,* XII–XIV, *The nineteenth century.* Cambridge, 1916–17.

3 Monographs

(See also sec. X, pt. 3, sec. XII, pt. 3, and sec. XIII, pt. 3, above.)

2220 *Adam & Charles Black, 1807–1957; some chapters in the history of a publishing house.* 1957.
2221 Albee, Ernest. *A history of English utilitarianism.* 2nd ed., 1957.
2222 Alexander, Edward. *Matthew Arnold and John Stuart Mill.* 1965.
2223 Anschutz, Richard P. *The philosophy of J. S. Mill.* Oxford, 1953.
2224 Appleman, Philip, William A. Madden and Michael Wolff (eds.). *1859: entering an age of crisis.* Bloomington, Ind., 1959. An interdisciplinary collection of essays on all aspects of the Victorian *annus mirabilis.*
2225 Armytage, Walter H. G. *The civic universities: aspects of a British tradition.* 1955.
2226 Ashton, Thomas S. *Economic and social investigations in Manchester, 1833–1933.* 1934. A history of the Manchester Statistical Society, with an index of reports and papers.
2227 Ausubel, Herman, J. Bartlet Brebner and Erling Hunt (eds.). *Some modern historians of Britain.* New York, 1951.
2228 Bell, Henry E. *Maitland: a critical examination and reassessment.* 1965.
2229 Benn, Alfred W. *The history of English rationalism in the nineteenth century.* 1906, 2 vols.
2230 Bevington, Merle M. *The Saturday Review, 1855–1868.* New York, 1941.
2231 Black, R. D. Collison. *Economic thought and the Irish question, 1817–1870.* Cambridge, 1960. Includes an extensive bibliography.
2232 —— *The Statistical and Social Inquiry Society of Ireland, centenary volume, 1847–1947.* Dublin, 1947. Research and thought which preceded the Land Acts.
2233 Blaug, Mark. *Ricardian economics; a historical study.* New Haven, 1958.
2234 Brown, Alan W. *The Metaphysical Society: Victorian minds in conflict 1869–1880.* New York, 1947. A good study of an important group.
2235 Buckley, Jerome H. *The triumph of time: a study of the Victorian concepts of time, history, progress, and decadence.* Cambridge, Mass., 1966.
2236 —— *The Victorian temper: a study in literary culture.* Cambridge, Mass., 1951. An important study of the 'moral aesthetic'.

2237 Burrow, John W. *Evolution and society: a study in Victorian social theory.* 1966.
2238 Caine, Sydney. *The history of the foundation of the London School of Economics and Political Science.* 1963.
2239 Cameron, James R. *Frederic William Maitland and the history of English law.* Norman, Okla., 1961.
2240 Clarke, Martin L. *Classical education in Britain, 1500–1900.* Cambridge, 1959.
2241 Cole, George D. H. *A history of socialist thought,* I, *The forerunners 1789–1850,* II, *Marxism and anarchism 1850–1890,* III, *The second international 1889–1910.* 1953–63. A major study.
2242 Cole, Margaret I. (ed.). *The Webbs and their work.* 1949.
2243 Connell, William F. *The educational thought and influence of Matthew Arnold.* 1950.
2244 Cowling, Maurice. *Mill and liberalism.* Cambridge, 1963. A hostile treatment.
2245 Cruse, Amy. *The Victorians and their books.* 1935.
2246 Culler, A. Dwight. *The imperial intellect; a study of Newman's educational ideal.* 1956.
2247 Curtis, Lewis P., Jr. *Anglo-Saxons and Celts: a study of anti-Irish prejudice in Victorian England* (Studies in British History and Culture, II). Bridgeport, Conn., 1968.
2248 Davidson, William L. *Political thought in England: the utilitarians from Bentham to J. S. Mill.* 1915.
2249 Davie, George E. *The democratic intellect: Scotland and her universities in the nineteenth century.* Edinburgh, 1961.
2250 Davies, Hugh S. (ed.). *The English mind: studies in the English moralists presented to Basil Willey.* Cambridge, 1964. Includes essays on Coleridge and the Victorians, Newman and the Romantic sensibility, J. S. Mill, and Arnold and the Continental idea.
2251 Decker, Clarence R. *The Victorian conscience.* New York, 1952. The relation of art and morality.
2252 Dunsheath, Percy and Margaret Miller. *Convocation in the University of London: the first hundred years.* 1958.
2253 *The Economist, 1843–1943: a centenary volume.* 1943.
2254 Eliot, Thomas S. *Knowledge and experience in the philosophy of F. H. Bradley.* 1964. A dissertation written in 1916.
2255 Ellegård, Alvar. *Darwin and the general reader; the reception of Darwin's theory of evolution in the British periodical press, 1859–1872.* Göteborg, 1958. A model study in intellectual history.
2256 —— *The readership of the periodical press in mid-Victorian Britain.* Göteborg, 1957. An excellent and important study.
2257 Eshag, Eprime. *From Marshall to Keynes; an essay on the monetary theory of the Cambridge school.* Oxford, 1963.
2258 Everett, Edwin M. *The party of humanity: the Fortnightly Review and its contributors 1865–1874.* Chapel Hill, N.C., 1939.
2259 Eversley, David E. C. *Social theories of fertility and the Malthusian debate.* Oxford, 1959.
2260 Faber, Richard. *Beaconsfield and Bolingbroke.* 1961. An essay in political thought.
2261 Fain, John T. *Ruskin and the economists.* Nashville, 1956.
2262 Fetter, Frank W. *Development of British monetary orthodoxy, 1797–1875.* Cambridge, Mass., 1965.
2263 Forbes, Duncan. *The liberal Anglican idea of history.* Cambridge, 1952.
2264 Fox Bourne, Henry R. *English newspapers; chapters in the history of journalism.* 1887, 2 vols.
2265 Fremantle, Anne. *This little band of prophets: the story of the gentle Fabians.* 1960.
2266 Gibb, Mildred A. and Frank Beckwith. *The Yorkshire Post: two centuries.* Leeds, 1954.
2267 Gooch, George P. *History and historians in the nineteenth century.* 2nd ed., 1952.

2268 Grampp, William D. *The Manchester school of economics*. Stanford, 1960.
2269 Green, Frederick C. *A comparative view of French and British civilisation (1850–1870)*. 1965.
2270 Green, Vivian H. H. *Oxford common room: a study of Lincoln College and Mark Pattison*. 1957.
2271 Greene, John C. *The death of Adam: evolution and its impact on Western thought*. Ames, Ia., 1959.
2272 Griffin, John R. *The intellectual milieu of Lord Macaulay*. Ottawa, 1964.
2273 Hamburger, Joseph. *Intellectuals in politics: John Stuart Mill and the philosophic radicals* (Yale Studies in Political Science, XIV). New Haven, 1965.
2274 Havard, William C. *Henry Sidgwick and later utilitarian political philosophy*. Gainesville, Fla., 1959.
2275 Hearnshaw, Fossey J. C. (ed.). *The social and political ideas of some representative thinkers of the Victorian age*. 1930.
2276 Himmelfarb, Gertrude. *Victorian minds*. New York, 1968. Includes studies of J. S. Mill, Acton, Leslie Stephen, Bagehot and J. A. Froude.
2277 *The history of 'The Times'*. 1935–48, 4 vols. in 5.
2278 Holloway, John. *The Victorian sage: studies in argument*. 1953. Examines Carlyle, Disraeli, George Eliot, Newman, Arnold and Hardy.
2279 Horn, David B. *A short history of the University of Edinburgh, 1556–1889*. Edinburgh, 1967.
2280 Houghton, Walter E. *The Victorian frame of mind*. New Haven, 1957. Erudite and penetrating analysis of the Victorian mentality through its leading literary figures.
2281 Howey, Richard S. *The rise of the marginal utility school, 1870–1889*. Lawrence, Kans., 1960.
2282 Hutchison, Terence W. *A review of economic doctrines, 1870–1929*. Oxford, 1953.
2283 *Ideas and beliefs of the Victorians; an historic revaluation of the Victorian age*. 1949. A symposium of radio talks.
2284 Jackson, Holbrook. *The eighteen-nineties; a review of art and ideas at the close of the nineteenth century*. 2nd ed., 1927. Still the best study of the period.
2285 Joad, Cyril E. M. (ed.). *Shaw and society; an anthology and a symposium*. 1953.
2286 Kauder, Emil. *A history of marginal utility theory*. Princeton, 1966.
2287 Kunitz, Stanley J. and Howard Haycraft (eds.). *British authors of the nineteenth century*. New York, 1936. A biographical dictionary.
2288 Ladd, Henry A. *The Victorian morality of art; an analysis of Ruskin's esthetic*. New York, 1932.
2289 Lawrence, Elwood P. *Henry George in the British Isles*. East Lansing, Mich., 1957.
2290 Le Chevalier, Charles. *Ethique et idéalisme, le courant néo-hégélien en Angleterre, Bernard Bosanquet et ses amis*. Paris, 1963.
2291 Link, Robert G. *English theories of economic fluctuations, 1815–1848*. New York, 1959.
2292 Lippincott, Benjamin E. *Victorian critics of democracy*. Minneapolis, 1938.
2293 MacCunn, John. *Six radical thinkers: Bentham, J. S. Mill, Cobden, Carlyle, Mazzini, T. H. Green*. 1907.
2294 McGrath, Fergal. *The consecration of learning: lectures on Newman's idea of a university*. Dublin, 1962.
2295 —— *Newman's university: idea and reality*. Dublin, 1951. A good history of the Catholic University of Dublin.
2296 McPherson, Robert G. *Theory of higher education in nineteenth-century England*. Athens, Ga., 1959.
2297 Majumdar, Tapas. *The measurement of utility*. 1958. Extensive treatment of Marshall.
2298 Mallet, Charles E. *A history of the University of Oxford*, III. 1927. The standard work.
2299 Marchand, Leslie A. *The Athenaeum: a mirror of Victorian culture*. Chapel Hill, N.C., 1941.

2300 Massingham, Harold J. and Hugh (eds.). *The great Victorians.* 1932. Numerous sketches of significant figures.
2301 Maxwell, Constantia. *A history of Trinity College, Dublin, 1591–1892.* Dublin, 1946.
2302 Milne, Alan J. M. *The social philosophy of English idealism.* 1962. On Bradley, Green and Bosanquet.
2303 Moody, Theodore W. and James C. Beckett. *Queen's Belfast, 1845–1949: the history of a university.* 1959, 2 vols.
2304 Morgan, Charles. *The house of Macmillan, 1843–1943.* 1943.
2305 Morison, Stanley. *The English newspaper 1622–1932.* Cambridge, 1932.
2306 Neff, Emery. *Carlyle and Mill: an introduction to Victorian thought.* New York, 1926. An important study.
2307 Nowell-Smith, Simon. *The house of Cassell, 1848–1958.* 1958.
2308 Ogilvie, Robert M. *Latin and Greek: a history of the influence of the classics on English life from 1600 to 1918.* 1964.
2309 Oliphant, Margaret O. and Mary Porter. *Annals of a publishing house, I–II, William Blackwood and his sons. Their magazine and friends, III, John Blackwood.* Edinburgh, 1897–8.
2310 Pankhurst, Richard K. P. *The Saint Simonians Mill and Carlyle; a preface to modern thought.* 1957.
2311 Pappe, Helmut O. *John Stuart Mill and the Harriet Taylor myth.* Parkville, S. A., 1960. De-emphasizes the influence of Harriet on Mill; contradicts (2191).
2312 Pease, Edward R. *The history of the Fabian Society.* 2nd ed., 1925. An official history.
2313 Penniman, Thomas K. *A hundred years of anthropology.* 1935.
2314 Pinto-Duschinsky, Michael. *The political thought of Lord Salisbury, 1854–68.* 1967.
2315 Price, Richard G. G. *A history of Punch.* 1957.
2316 Pucelle, Jean. *L'Idéalisme en Angleterre, de Coleridge à Bradley: être et penser.* Neuchâtel, 1955.
2317 —— *La Nature et l'esprit dans la philosophie de T. H. Green: la renaissance de l'idéalisme en Angleterre au XIXe siècle.* Louvain, 1961–5, 2 vols.
2318 Read, Donald. *Press and people, 1790–1850: opinion in three English cities.* 1961. The cities are Manchester, Leeds and Sheffield.
2319 Rees, John C. *Mill and his early critics.* Leicester, 1956.
2320 Robbins, Lionel C., Baron. *The theory of economic policy in English classical political economy.* 1952.
2321 Robertson Scott, John W. *The story of the Pall Mall Gazette, of its first editor Frederick Greenwood and of its founder George Murray Smith.* 1950.
2322 Roe, Frederick W. *The social philosophy of Carlyle and Ruskin.* 1922.
2323 Roll-Hansen, Diderik. *The Academy 1869–1879; Victorian intellectuals in revolt.* Copenhagen, 1957.
2324 Rosenbaum, Robert A. *Earnest Victorians.* New York, 1961. Sketches of Ashley, Newman, Browning, Rossetti, Darwin and Gordon.
2325 Samuels, Warren T. *The classical theory of economic policy.* Cleveland, 1966.
2326 Schilling, Bernard N. *Human dignity and the great Victorians.* New York, 1946.
2327 Schuyler, Robert L. (ed.). *Frederic William Maitland, historian.* Berkeley, 1960.
2328 Simon, Walter M. *European positivism in the nineteenth century: an essay in intellectual history.* Ithaca, N.Y., 1963.
2329 Sparrow, John. *Mark Pattison and the idea of a university.* 1967.
2330 Spielmann, Marion H. *The history of 'Punch'.* 1895.
2331 Spiller, Gustav. *The ethical movement in Great Britain; a documentary history.* 1934.
2332 Steed, H. Wickham. *The press.* Harmondsworth, 1938.
2333 Stephen, Leslie. *The English utilitarians, III, John Stuart Mill.* 1900.
2334 Thomas, William B. *The story of the 'Spectator'.* 1928.
2335 Thompson, James W. *A history of historical writing, II.* New York, 1942.
2336 Thompson, Paul. *The work of William Morris.* 1967.

2337 Thrall, Miriam M. H. *Rebellious Fraser's: Nol Yorke's magazine in the days of Maginn, Thackeray and Carlyle.* New York, 1934.
2338 Tillyard, Alfred I. *A history of university reform from 1800 A.D. to the present time* ... Cambridge, 1913.
2339 Ulam, Adam B. *Philosophical foundations of English socialism.* Cambridge, Mass., 1951.
2340 Viner, Jacob. *The long view and the short: studies in economic theory and policy.* Glencoe, Ill., 1958. Includes essays on Mill and Marshall.
2341 Ward, William R. *Victorian Oxford.* 1965.
2342 Willey, Basil. *More nineteenth century studies, a group of honest doubters.* 1956.
2343 —— *Nineteenth century studies, Coleridge to Matthew Arnold.* 1949. Major contributions to intellectual history, with emphasis on religious aspects.
2344 Williams, Raymond. *Culture and society, 1780–1950.* 1958. The relation of intellectual history to mass culture.
2345 —— *The long revolution.* 1961. The development of mass culture and communications.
2346 Winstanley, Dennis A. *Early Victorian Cambridge.* Cambridge, 1940.
2347 —— *Later Victorian Cambridge.* Cambridge, 1947.
2348 Woods, Thomas. *Poetry and philosophy: a study in the thought of John Stuart Mill.* 1961.
2349 Woodward, Frances J. *The doctor's disciples: a study of four pupils of Arnold of Rugby—Stanley, Gell, Clough and William Arnold.* 1954.
2350 Young, George M. *Victorian essays,* ed. W. D. Handcock. 1962. Brilliant essays by the wisest of Victorian scholars.

4 Biographies
(See also sec. XII, pt. 4, above.)

2351 Abbott, Evelyn and Lewis Campbell. *The life and letters of Benjamin Jowett, M.A., Master of Balliol College, Oxford.* 1897, 2 vols.
2352 Annan, Noel G. *Leslie Stephen: his thought and character in relation to his time.* 1951.
2353 Auchmuty, James J. *Lecky.* Dublin, 1945.
2354 Benson, Arthur C. *Walter Pater.* 1906.
2355 Britton, Karl. *John Stuart Mill; an introduction to the life and teaching of a great pioneer of modern social philosophy and logic.* 1953.
2356 Brodie, Fawn M. *The Devil drives: a life of Sir Richard Burton.* New York, 1967.
2357 Brooks, Constance. *Antonio Panizzi, scholar and patriot.* Manchester, 1931.
2358 Buchan, Alastair. *The spare chancellor; the life of Walter Bagehot.* 1959.
2359 Clarke, Martin L. *George Grote, a biography.* 1962.
2360 Cole, Margaret I. *Beatrice Webb.* 1945.
2361 Cook, Edward. *Delane of the Times.* 1916.
2362 —— *The life of John Ruskin.* 1911, 2 vols.
2363 Cranston, Maurice. *John Stuart Mill.* 1958. A short sketch, with bibliography.
2364 Dasent, Arthur I. *John Thadeus Delane, editor of 'The Times'; his life and correspondence.* 1908, 2 vols.
2365 Duncan, David. *Life and letters of Herbert Spencer.* 1908, 2 vols.
2366 Dunn, Waldo H. *James Anthony Froude: a biography.* Oxford, 1961–3, 2 vols.
2367 Ervine, St John G. *Bernard Shaw: his life, work, and friends.* 1956.
2368 Evans, Joan. *John Ruskin.* 1954.
2369 Faber, Geoffrey. *Jowett, a portrait with background.* 1957.
2370 Fisher, Herbert A. L. *James Bryce (Viscount Bryce of Dechmont, O.M.).* 1927, 2 vols.
2371 Froude, James A. *Thomas Carlyle: a history of his life in London, 1834–1881.* 1884, 2 vols. This book was the centre of a controversy when it was published, on account of its inaccuracies and its excessive frankness.
2372 Fyfe, H. Hamilton. *Northcliffe, an intimate biography.* 1930.
2373 Giles, Frank. *A prince of journalists: the life and times of De Blowitz.* 1962.
2374 Hammond, John L. *C. P. Scott of the 'Manchester Guardian'.* 1934.

2375 Henderson, Archibald. *George Bernard Shaw: man of the century*. New York, 1956. The most comprehensive biography.
2376 Henderson, Philip. *William Morris: his life, work, and friends*. 1967. A substantial study.
2377 Hirst, Francis W. *Early life and letters of John Morley*. 1927, 2 vols.
2378 Hobson, John A. *John Ruskin, social reformer*. 1898. Still useful.
2379 Hutchinson, Horatio G. *Life of Sir John Lubbock, Lord Avebury*. 1914, 2 vols.
2380 Irvine, William. *Walter Bagehot*. 1939.
2381 Kubie, Nora B. *Road to Nineveh: the adventures and excavations of Sir Austen Henry Layard*. New York, 1964.
2382 Lecky, Elisabeth. *A memoir of the Right Hon. William Edward Hartpole Lecky* . . . 1909.
2383 McDowell, Robert B. *Alice Stopford Green: a passionate historian*. Dublin, 1967.
2384 Mack, Edward C. and Walter H. G. Armytage. *Thomas Hughes: a life of the author of Tom Brown's Schooldays*. 1952.
2385 Mackail, John W. *The life of William Morris*. 2nd ed., 1950.
2386 Maitland, Frederic W. *The life and letters of Leslie Stephen*. 1906.
2387 Miller, Edward. *Prince of librarians: the life and times of Antonio Panizzi of the British Museum*. 1967.
2388 Morris, May. *William Morris, artist, writer, socialist*. Oxford, 1936, 2 vols.
2389 Muggeridge, Kitty and Ruth Adam. *Beatrice Webb: a life, 1858–1943*. 1967.
2390 Müller, Georgina A. *The life and letters of the Right Honourable Friedrich Max Müller*. 1902, 2 vols.
2391 Neff, Emery. *Carlyle*. 1932.
2392 Nethercot, Arthur H. *The first five lives of Annie Besant*. 1961.
2393 Nettleship, Richard L. *Memoir of Thomas Hill Green, late fellow of Balliol College, Oxford, and Whyte's Professor of Moral Philosophy in the University of Oxford*. 1906.
2394 Packe, Michael St J. *The life of John Stuart Mill*. 1954.
2395 Paul, Herbert. *The life of Froude*. 1905.
2396 Pound, Reginald and Geoffrey Harmsworth. *Northcliffe*. 1959.
2397 Quennell, Peter C. *John Ruskin: the portrait of a prophet*. 1949.
2398 Richter, Melvin. *The politics of conscience: T. H. Green and his age*. 1964. An important study.
2399 Robbins, Lionel C., Baron. *Robert Torrens and the evolution of classical economics*. 1958.
2400 St Aubyn, Giles. *A Victorian eminence: the life and works of Henry Thomas Buckle*. 1958.
2401 St John-Stevas, Norman. *Walter Bagehot: a study of his life and thought together with a selection from his political writings*. 1959.
2402 Simey, Thomas S. and Margaret B. *Charles Booth, social scientist*. 1960.
2403 Smiles, Aileen. *Samuel Smiles and his surroundings*. 1956.
2404 Stephen, William R. W. *The life and letters of Edward A. Freeman*. 1895, 2 vols. Important for historiography.
2405 Thompson, Edward P. *William Morris: romantic to revolutionary*. 1955. A massive and definitive biography.
2406 Thompson, Laurence. *Robert Blatchford: portrait of an Englishman*. 1951.
2407 Thomson, Mark A. *Macaulay* (Historical Association, General Series, XLII). 1959. A short pamphlet.
2408 Trevelyan, George O. *The life and letters of Lord Macaulay*. 2nd ed., 1908.
2409 Trilling, Lionel. *Matthew Arnold*. New York, 1939. A major study.
2410 Tsuzuki, Chūshichi. *H. M. Hyndman and British socialism*, ed. Henry Pelling. 1961.
2411 —— *The life of Eleanor Marx, 1855–1898*. 1967.
2412 Wallace, Elisabeth. *Goldwin Smith, Victorian liberal*. Toronto, 1957.
2413 Webb, Robert K. *Harriet Martineau: radical Victorian*. 1960.
2414 West, Alick. *'A good man fallen among Fabians'*. 1950. A life of George Bernard Shaw.
2415 Williams, Gertrude M. *The passionate pilgrim; a life of Annie Besant*. 1932.
2416 Wilson, David A. *Life of Thomas Carlyle*. 1923–34, 6 vols.
2417 Wollheim, Richard. *F. H. Bradley*. 1959.

5 Articles
(See also sec. x, pt. 5, and sec. xii, pt. 5, above.)

2418 Altick, Richard D. 'English publishing and the mass audience in 1852', *Studies in Bibliography*, **6** (1954), 3–24.

2419 —— 'The sociology of authorship: the social origins, education and occupations of 1,100 British writers, 1800–1935', *Bulletin of the New York Public Library*, **66** (June 1962), 389–404.

2420 Annan, Noel G. 'The intellectual aristocracy', in John H. Plumb (ed.). *Studies in social history: a tribute to G. M. Trevelyan*. 1955, pp. 243–87. An excellent study of the familial relationships of leading intellectuals.

2421 Banks, Joseph A. and Olive. 'The Bradlaugh–Besant trial and the English newspapers', *Population Studies*, **8** (July 1954), 22–34.

2422 Baylen, Joseph O. 'W. T. Stead and the Boer war: the irony of idealism' *Canadian Historical Review*, **40** (Dec. 1959), 304–14.

2423 Bibby, Cyril. 'Thomas Henry Huxley and university development', *VS*, **2** (Dec. 1958), 97–116.

2424 Bicknell, John W. 'Leslie Stephen's "English Thought in the Eighteenth Century": a tract for the times', *VS*, **6** (Dec. 1962), 103–20.

2425 Black, R. D. Collison. 'Jevons and Cairnes', *Economica*, **27** (Aug. 1960), 214–32. Includes correspondence, 1863–74.

2426 Blaug, Mark. 'The classical economists and the Factory Acts—a re-examination', *Quarterly Journal of Economics*, **73** (May 1958), 211–26.

2427 Burrow, John W. 'Evolution and anthropology in the 1860's: the Anthropological Society of London, 1863–71', *VS*, **7** (Dec. 1963), 137–54.

2428 —— 'The uses of philology in Victorian England', in *Id. & Inst.*, pp. 180–204.

2429 Cadogan, Peter. 'Harney and Engels', *IRSH*, **10** (pt. 1, 1965), 66–104.

2430 Checkland, Sydney G. 'The Birmingham economists, 1815–1850', *EcHR*, 2nd ser., **1** (no. 1, 1948), 1–19.

2431 —— 'Economic opinion in England as Jevons found it', *The Manchester School of Economic and Social Studies*, **19** (May 1951), 143–69.

2432 Clark, George S. R. Kitson. 'The romantic element, 1830 to 1850', in John H. Plumb (ed.). *Studies in social history: a tribute to G. M. Trevelyan.* 1955, pp. 211–39.

2433 Coates, Willson H. 'Benthamism, laissez-faire and collectivism', *JHI*, **11** (June 1950), 357–63.

2434 Collins, James. 'Darwin's impact on philosophy', *Thought*, **34** (Summer 1959), 185–248. An impressive monograph.

2435 Crowe, M. B. 'Huxley and humanism', *Studies*, **49** (Autumn 1960), 249–60.

2436 DeLaura, David J. 'Pater and Newman: the road to the "nineties"', *VS*, **10** (Sept. 1966), 39–69.

2437 Eisen, Sydney. 'Frederic Harrison and the religion of humanity', *South Atlantic Quarterly*, **66** (Autumn 1967), 574–90.

2438 —— 'Herbert Spencer and the spectre of Comte', *JBS*, **7** (Nov. 1967), 48–67.

2439 —— 'Huxley and the positivists', *VS*, **7** (June 1964), 337–58.

2440 Ellegård, Alvar. 'Public opinion and the press: reactions to Darwinism', *JHI*, **19** (June 1958), 379–87.

2441 Fetter, Frank W. 'Economic controversy in the British reviews, 1802–1850', *Economica*, **32** (Nov. 1965), 424–37.

2442 —— 'Robert Torrens: Colonel of Marines and political economist', *Economica*, **29** (May 1962), 152–65.

2443 Fletcher, Ian. 'The 1890's: a lost decade', *VS*, **4** (June 1961), 345–54.

2444 Fowler, William S. 'The influence of idealism upon state provision of education', *VS*, **4** (June 1961), 337–44.

2445 Gerber, Helmut E. 'The nineties: beginning, end, or transition?', in Richard Ellmann (ed.). *Edwardians and late Victorians* (English Institute Essays, 1959). New York, 1960, pp. 50–79.

2446 Gordon, Barry J. 'Say's law, effective demand, and the contemporary

British periodicals, 1820–1850', *Economica*, **32** (Nov. 1965), 438–46. Attacks on Ricardo.

2447 Griest, Guinevere L. 'A Victorian leviathan: Mudie's Select Library', *Nineteenth-Century Fiction*, **20** (Sept. 1965), 103–26.

2448 Hague, Douglas C. 'Alfred Marshall and the competitive firm', *Economic Journal*, **68** (Dec. 1958), 673–90.

2449 Halsted, John B. 'Walter Bagehot on toleration', *JHI*, **19** (Jan. 1958), 119–28.

2450 Harrison, Royden. 'E. S. Beesly and Karl Marx', *IRSH*, **4** (pts. 1–2, 1959), 22–58, 208–38. A valuable article on the influence of the positivists on socialism, with extracts from correspondence.

2451 Houghton, Walter E. 'Victorian anti-intellectualism', *JHI*, **13** (June 1952), 291–313.

2452 Howat, G. M. B. 'The nineteenth-century history text-book', *British Journal of Educational Studies*, **13** (May 1965), 147–59.

2453 Irvine, William. 'George Bernard Shaw and Karl Marx', *JEcH*, **6** (May 1946), 53–72.

2454 Jones, Howard Mumford. 'The comic spirit and Victorian sanity', in Joseph E. Baker (ed.). *The reinterpretation of Victorian literature*. Princeton, 1950, pp. 20–32. A defence of the Victorians against critics of their self-importance.

2455 Jump, John D. 'Weekly reviewing in the eighteen-fifties', *Review of English Studies*, **24** (Jan. 1948), 42–57.

2456 Kissane, James. 'Victorian mythology', *VS*, **6** (Sept. 1962), 5–28. Victorian attitudes to and study of mythology.

2457 Kittrell, Edward R. '"Laissez faire" in English classical economics', *JHI*, **27** (Oct. 1966), 610–20. Uses of the word.

2458 Levy, F. J. 'The founding of the Camden Society', *VS*, **7** (Mar. 1964), 295–305.

2459 Lowenthal, Leo and Ina Lawson. 'The debate on cultural standards in nineteenth century England', *Social Research*, **30** (Winter 1963), 417–33.

2460 McCartney, Donal. 'Lecky's "Leaders of Public Opinion in Ireland"', *IHS*, **14** (Sept. 1964), 119–41.

2461 Mack, Mary Peter. 'The Fabians and utilitarianism', *JHI*, **16** (Jan. 1955), 76–88.

2462 MacRae, Donald G. 'Darwinism and the social sciences', in Samuel A. Barnett (ed.). *A century of Darwin*. 1958, pp. 296–312.

2463 Mason, J. F. A. 'The third Marquess of Salisbury and the Saturday Review', *BIHR*, **34** (May 1961), 36–54.

2464 Maurer, Oscar. 'Froude and *Fraser's Magazine*, 1860–1874', *University of Texas Studies in English*, **28** (1949), 213–43.

2465 —— '"My squeamish public": some problems of Victorian magazine publishers and editors', *Studies in Bibliography*, **12** (1959), 21–40.

2466 Melitz, Jack. 'Sidgwick's theory of international values', *Economic Journal*, **73** (Sept. 1963), 431–41.

2467 Miller, Kenneth E. 'John Stuart Mill's theory of international relations', *JHI*, **22** (Oct. 1961), 493–514.

2468 Mulvey, Helen. 'The historian Lecky: opponent of Irish home rule', *VS*, **1** (June 1958), 337–51.

2469 Murphree, Idus L. 'The evolutionary anthropologists: the progress of mankind: the concepts of progress and culture in the thought of John Lubbock, Edward B. Tylor, and Lewis H. Morgan', *Proceedings of the American Philosophical Society*, **105** (1961), 265–300.

2470 Nicholls, David. 'Positive liberty, 1880–1914', *American Political Science Review*, **56** (Mar. 1962), 114–28. The clash between 'negative' and 'positive' liberals.

2471 Nicholson, Joseph S. 'The British economists', in *CMH*, x, 763–84.

2472 O'Brien, D. P. 'The transition in Torrens' monetary thought', *Economica*, **32** (Aug. 1965), 269–301.

2473 Odom, Herbert H. 'Generalizations on race in nineteenth-century physical anthropology', *Isis*, **58** (Spring 1967), 4–18.

2474 Passmore, John. 'Darwin's impact on British metaphysics', *VS*, **3** (Sept. 1959), 41–54.

2475 Peckham, Morse. 'Darwin and Darwinisticism', *VS*, **3** (Sept. 1959), 19–40. On the genuineness of the uses of Darwin.

2476 Plumb, John H. 'Thomas Babington Macaulay', in *Men and centuries: essays.* 1963, pp. 250–66.

2477 Pursell, G. 'Unity in the thought of Alfred Marshall', *Quarterly Journal of Economics*, **72** (Nov. 1958), 588–600.

2478 Randall, John H. 'The changing impact of Darwin on philosophy', *JHI*, **22** (Oct. 1961), 435–62.

2479 —— 'John Stuart Mill and the working-out of empiricism', *JHI*, **26** (Jan. 1965), 59–88.

2480 —— 'T. H. Green: the development of English thought from J. S. Mill to F. H. Bradley', *JHI*, **27** (Apr. 1966), 217–44.

2481 Richter, Melvin. 'T. H. Green and his audience: liberalism as a surrogate faith', *Review of Politics*, **18** (Oct. 1956), 444–72.

2482 Roach, John. 'Liberalism and the Victorian intelligentsia', *Camb. Hist. J.*, **13** (no. 1, 1957), 58–81.

2483 —— 'Victorian universities and the national intelligentsia', *VS*, **2** (Dec. 1959), 131–50.

2484 Robson, Robert. 'Trinity College in the age of Peel', in *Id. & Inst.*, pp. 312–35.

2485 Rodgers, Brian. 'The Social Science Association, 1857–1886', *The Manchester School of Economic and Social Studies*, **20** (Sept. 1952), 283–310.

2486 Sandelius, Walter E. 'Liberalism and the political philosophy of Thomas Hill Green', in Orel, Harold and George J. Worth (eds.). *Six studies in nineteenth-century English literature and thought.* Lawrence, Kans., 1962, pp. 39–53.

2487 Schapiro, J. Salwyn. 'Thomas Carlyle, prophet of fascism', *JMH*, **17** (June 1945), 97–115.

2488 Schwartz, Pedro. 'John Stuart Mill and laissez-faire: London water', *Economica*, **33** (Feb. 1966), 71–83.

2489 Simon, Walter M. 'Auguste Comte's English disciples', *VS*, **8** (Dec. 1964), 161–72.

2490 —— 'Herbert Spencer and the "social organism"', *JHI*, **21** (Apr. 1960), 294–9.

2491 Simpson, George E. 'Darwin and "social Darwinism"', *Antioch Review*, **19** (Spring 1959), 33–45. The entire issue is devoted to the Darwin centennial.

2492 Smellie, Kingsley B. 'Sir Henry Maine', *Economica*, **8** (Mar. 1928), 64–94.

2493 Sorenson, L. R. 'Some classical economists, laissez-faire, and the Factory Acts', *JEcH*, **12** (Summer 1952), 247–62. See also (2426).

2494 Spiegelberg, Herbert. '"Accident of birth": a non-utilitarian motif in Mill's philosophy', *JHI*, **22** (Oct. 1961), 475–92.

2495 Stigler, George J. 'Bernard Shaw, Sidney Webb, and the theory of Fabian socialism', *Proceedings of the American Philosophical Society*, **103** (1959), 469–75.

2496 Swart, Koenraad W. '"Individualism" in the mid-nineteenth century (1826–1860)', *JHI*, **23** (Jan. 1962), 77–90. Use of the word by several writers, including Mill and Carlyle.

2497 Tucker, Albert V. 'W. H. Mallock and late Victorian conservatism', *University of Toronto Quarterly*, **31** (Jan. 1962), 223–41.

2498 Wallace, Elisabeth. 'The political ideas of the Manchester school', *University of Toronto Quarterly*, **29** (Jan. 1960), 122–38.

2499 Wolff, Michael. 'Charting the golden stream: thoughts on a directory of Victorian periodicals', in John M. Robson (ed.). *Editing nineteenth-century texts.* Toronto, 1966, pp. 37–59. Important for further research on periodicals.

2500 —— 'The uses of context: aspects of the 1860's', *VS*, **9** (Supplement, 1966), 47–63. An interdisciplinary approach to Victorian studies.

INDEX OF AUTHORS, EDITORS, AND TRANSLATORS

[Numbers are entry numbers except when otherwise specified]

INDEX OF AUTHORS, ETC.

Hirst, Francis W., 216, 1274-5, 1333, 2377
Hitchcock, Henry-Russell, 2086, 2124, 2179-80
Hjelholt, Holger, 766
Hobhouse, Christopher, 983
Hobsbawm, Eric J., 319, 984-5, 1443-5
Hobson, John A., 517, 2378
Hodder, Edwin, 518
Hoffman, Ross J., 1276
Hoffmann, Walter G., 1277-8
Hogben, Lancelot T., 1131, 1602
Hogg, Ethel, 1094
Holdsworth, William S., 145
Hole, Christina, 986
Holland, Bernard H., 519
Hollingsworth, Thomas H., 1136
Hollis, Christopher, 987
Hollis, Patricia, 641
Holloway, John, 2278
Holloway, S. W. F., 1137
Holmes, J. Derek, 2011, 2034-5
Holt, Edgar, 1727
Holt, Raymond V., 1843
Holyoake, George J., 1279
Hooker, Elizabeth R., 1514
Hooykaas, Reijer, 1603, 1681
Hopkins, S. V., 1331
Hopkinson, Edward C., 1720
Hopley, I. B., 1678-80
Horn, David B., 2279
Hornby, George C., 1840
Horne, H. Oliver, 1280
Hoskin, Michael A., 1663, 1689
Hoskins, George O., 1219
Hoskins, William G., 988, 1515-16
Hough, Richard, 1728
Houghton, Walter E., 59, 2280, 2451
Houston, George, 1517
Hovell, Mark, 400
Howard, Christopher H. D., 310, 320, 652-4, 767, 832-3
Howard, Derek L., 187
Howard, Michael, 1760
Howarth, Osbert J. R., 1604
Howat, G. M. B., 2452
Howe, Ellic, 1281
Howe, George F. 15
Howey, Richard S., 2281
Hubbard, Hesketh, 2087, 2125
Hugh, Father, 60
Hughes, Dorothea Price, 1961
Hughes, Edward, 274-6
Hughes, Emrys, 520
Hughes, George B., 2126
Hughes, Gervase, 2127
Hughes, Jonathan R. T., 1282, 1423, 1446-7
Hughes, Thomas P., 1448
Humphrey, Arthur W., 401, 1388
Humphreys, Betty V., 188

Hunt, Bishop C., 1283
Hunt, Edward H., 1541
Hunt, Erling, 2227
Hunt, W. Holman, 2128
Hurd, Douglas, 1729
Hurst, John F., 1844
Hurst, Michael C., 402-3, 655
Hussey, Christopher, 2167
Hutchings, Arthur, 2129
Hutchins, B. Leigh, 189
Hutchinson, Horace G., 321
Hutchinson, Horatio G., 2379
Hutchison, Keith, 1284
Hutchison, Terence W., 2282
Hutton, William H., 2193
Huxley, Francis, 1682
Huxley, Gervas, 1095
Huxley, Julian S., 1638, 1683
Huxley, Leonard, 1639-40
Hyams, Edward, 339
Hyde, Francis E., 1285-6
Hyde, Harford M., 2194
Hyndman, Henry M., 2195

Ihde, Aaron J., 1605
Ilbert, Courtenay P., 190
Ilchester, Giles S. H. Fox-Strangways, 6th Earl of, 989
Ilersic, Alfred R., 1287
Imlah, Albert H., 1288, 1449
Imlah, Ann G., 768
Ingham, S. M., 2036
Inglis, Kenneth S., 1845, 2037-9
Innes, John W., 990
Ironside, Robin, 2130
Irvine, William, 1606, 2380, 2453
Irwin, Raymond, 62

Jackman, William T., 1289
Jackson, Holbrook, 2284
Jackson, John A., 991
Jagow, Curt, 129
James, David, 1750
James, Robert R., 521-2
Jarman, Thomas L., 100, 1189
Jefferson, Margaret M., 834
Jeffery, James R., 921
Jefferys, James B., 1174, 1290-1, 1450
Jenkins, Hester, 1138
Jenkins, Robert T., 66
Jenkins, Roy, 523-4
Jenks, Edward, 191
Jenks, Leland H., 1292
Jennings, Louis L., 322
Jennings, William Ivor, 192, 198, 404
Jessop, Thomas E., 2215
Joad, Cyril E. M., 2285
John, Arthur H., 1293-4
Johnson, Franklyn A., 1730
Johnson, Leonard G., 525, 992
Johnston, John O., 1962, 1968